The Politics of Toleration in Modern Life

The Politics of Toleration in Modern Life

Edited by Susan Mendus

Duke University Press
Durham 2000

© in this edition Edinburgh University Press, 1999
Copyright in the individual contributions is retained by the authors

First published 1999 by
Edinburgh University Press
22 George Square, Edinburgh
and in 2000 by
Duke University Press, Durham, NC 27708-0660

Typeset in Linotype Bembo
by Hewer Text Limited, Edinburgh, and
printed and bound in Great Britain by
The University Press, Cambridge

Library of Congress Cataloging-in-Publication Data

The politics of toleration in modern life
/ edited by Susan Mendus.
     p.   cm.
   Includes index.
   ISBN 0-8223-2462-8 (cloth : alk. paper). – ISBN 0-8223-2498-9
(paper : alk. paper)
   1. Toleration.   I. Mendus, Susan.
JC571.P643   2000
179'.9--dc21   99-32392
                                                                    CIP

For Geoffrey Heselton and Nicholas Morrell
with thanks

Contents

Acknowledgements

Since 1980 the C. and J. B. Morrell Trust has funded research into toleration as a philosophical concept at the University of York. A major event in the calendar of the Morrell Studies Programme is the Annual Address, and this book consists of the texts of the Addresses delivered in the years 1988 to 1998. In addition to the Morrell Address, the Trust also funds studentships for the Masters degree in Political Philosophy (The Idea of Toleration), academic conferences, workshops and seminars. Both the University of York and the Politics Department are deeply indebted to the Trustees for their generous and sustained support of this programme of study.

My personal thanks go to all my colleagues in the Politics Department, but especially to my fellow political theorists: Alex Callinicos, David Edwards, Duncan Ivison, Matt Matravers and Peter Nicholson. That I can think of no better (and no happier) environment in which to do research in political philosophy is thanks to them. And I do thank them most warmly.

Until early 1995 John Horton was also my colleague, and Director of the Morrell Studies Programme. Both before and since his departure to the University of Keele, John has given unstinting support to the Morrell Studies Programme and without his efforts it would not have been possible to produce this collection.

Katy Fellows typed the text of the Addresses efficiently and with unfailing good humour. I am grateful to her and to Gill Pulpher, her predecessor as Morrell Secretary.

Finally, I would like to acknowledge my personal debt to two of the Trustees, Geoffrey Heselton and Nicholas Morrell, who have encouraged and supported me throughout the fifteen years of my involvement in the Morrell Studies Programme. Their support has meant a great deal to me, and I dedicate this book to Geoffrey and Nicholas, with warmest thanks.

Susan Mendus
University of York
August 1998

Notes on contributors

Garrett Fitzgerald was Taoiseach of Ireland from 1981 to 1982 and from 1982 to 1987. His autobiography, *All in a Life*, was published in 1991.

Christopher Hill is one of Britain's most distinguished historians. From 1938 to 1965 he was Fellow and Tutor in Modern History at Balliol College, Oxford, and Master of Balliol from 1965 to 1978. Professor Hill has written extensively on seventeenth-century English history and his books include: *The World Turned Upside Down, Milton and the English Revolution* and *Anti-Christ in Seventeenth Century England.*

George Carey was enthroned as 103rd Archbishop of Canterbury in 1991. He was previously Principal of Trinity College, Bristol, and Bishop of Bath and Wells.

Bernard Williams has been the occupant of both the Knightsbridge Chair of Philosophy at Cambridge and the White's Chair of Moral Philosophy at Oxford. He has written widely on problems of philosophy, both contemporary and historical, and his best-known works include: *Ethics and the Limits of Philosophy, Shame and Necessity* and *Descartes.*

Michael Ignatieff is a prominent broadcaster and writer. His book *Blood and Belonging* was written to accompany the BBC documentary series of the same title. He is also author of two novels, and of work in moral and political philosophy.

Helena Kennedy is a barrister, broadcaster and writer. She has been presenter of the BBC's *Heart of the Matter* and of *Hypotheticals*. Her book *Eve Was Framed*, a discussion of women and criminal justice, was published in 1992.

Julia Neuberger served as Rabbi at the South London Liberal Synagogue from 1977 to 1989, and chaired the Rabbinic Conference of the Union of Liberal and Progressive Synagogues from 1983 to 1985. She has been a member of the Human Fertilisation and Embryology Authority, and of the NHS Advisory Service. She has also written extensively on Judaism and her book *On Being Jewish* was published in 1996.

Alasdair MacIntyre is Arts and Sciences Professor of Philosophy at Duke University, having previously held academic appointments at the Universities of Notre Dame, Manchester, Oxford, Leeds and Essex. His work on moral and political philosophy includes: *After Virtue, Whose Justice? Which Rationality?* and *Three Rival Versions of Moral Enquiry*.

Chapter 1

My brother's keeper: the politics of intolerance
Susan Mendus

In his contribution to this volume, Michael Ignatieff draws attention
to what he calls 'the Cain and Abel Syndrome': the 'ironic fact that
intolerance between brothers is often stronger than that between
strangers'. He exemplifies his point through a discussion of the case of
Northern Ireland and notes that, despite the antagonism between
Catholic and Protestant communities, 'the two antagonists frequently
admit [that] no one understands the other as well as they do; they are
truly brother enemies.'[1] Moreover, the Irish case is far from unique.
Hostility between Russians and Ukranians, Serbs and Croats, Arabs
and Sephardi Jews are all exemplifications, to greater or lesser degree,
of the Cain and Abel Syndrome: the irony whereby those who know
most about each other, and differ least from each other, may yet be
most intolerant of each other.

The story of Cain and Abel can serve as a motif for this
collection as a whole. Each of the contributions was originally
delivered as a Morrell Memorial Address on Toleration, yet many
of the contributors focus on the causes of and remedies for
intolerance. And several identify precisely the ironic fact to which
Ignatieff draws our attention: that those who are closest – geo-
graphically, ethnically, religiously, and in many other ways – may
also be most divided.

There is, moreover, a second irony in the situation. This is that in
the modern world intolerance between 'brothers' co-exists uneasily
with increased solidarity between strangers. For, as Garrett Fitzgerald
points out in Chapter 2, the late twentieth century has seen a
remarkable growth in the sense of human solidarity. Fitzgerald writes:

the fact that the *concept* of international solidarity is now widely
accepted is immensely significant. This acceptance reflects one of the
most extraordinary transformations in human attitudes that has
occurred in history . . . During a period in which religion itself
has lost much ground, the gospel concept of every man being one's
neighbour has belatedly come to be quite widely accepted.[2]

In the late twentieth century, it seems, we are willing to acknowledge, against Cain, that we are our brother's keeper, at least in the
sense that we cannot slough off responsibility for poverty and
deprivation in other countries, however far-flung they may be.
Yet this willingness to see strangers as brothers sits ill with the fact
that those who are more nearly brothers engage in the civil war,
intra-state conflict, and ethnic cleansing which are the more shameful
hallmarks of late twentieth-century politics.

What, then, are the causes and what the remedies for this state of
affairs? Historically, discussions of toleration have often placed faith in
the possibility of reasoned resolutions to intolerance. John Locke's
Letter on Toleration is one of the earliest principled defences of
toleration, and J. W. Gough has noted that its importance springs
precisely from 'the orderliness and reasonableness and philosophical
temper' of its arguments.[3] The belief that the growth and application
of reason will usher in an era of increased toleration is widespread, but
the contributors to this volume give us pause for thought on that
point. They emphasise the political dimension of intolerance and its
recalcitrance to the operations of reason. Concomitantly, they
emphasise the significance of political responses to the problem of
intolerance, both historically and in the modern era. The Cain and
Abel syndrome is, at root, a political problem and one which must
therefore seek a political solution. But what kind of political solution
is appropriate? And why? On these questions, and as we shall see, the
contributors differ significantly, and here their different responses
reflect not merely different political commitments, but also different
philosophical allegiances. They subscribe to different views about the
proper role of the state (or of politics generally) in responding to the
fact of intolerance in the modern world, and they therefore advocate
different political policies for addressing intolerance.

What is contained or included in their definition/way of 'political'?

Causes of intolerance

With these preliminaries noted, we can move on to our central questions: what are the causes of intolerance and what are its remedies? As several of the contributors point out, toleration is distinct from mere indifference. We are genuinely tolerant of others only when we disapprove of them, or of their actions and beliefs, but nonetheless refrain from imposing our own view. As George Carey notes: 'people with no convictions are not being tolerant if they allow others their way, or if they acquiesce with the opinions of others. They are simply "indifferent" . . . *Indifference is not toleration.*'[4] So one necessary condition of toleration is the presence of disapproval or hostility.

This, however, raises an immediate problem, which is identified by Bernard Williams. It is that toleration appears to be, at one and the same time, necessary and impossible: 'we need to tolerate other people and their ways of life only in situations that make it very difficult to do so. Toleration, we may say, is required only for the intolerable. That is its basic problem.'[5] Enmity, hostility and antagonism are the necessary preconditions of toleration, but it is difficult to see why we should tolerate things which we find repellent or abhorrent, much less why we should count it a virtue so to do.

Moreover, both Carey and Williams concentrate on toleration with regard to the beliefs or opinions of others, but it is not only with respect to beliefs that problems of toleration arise, for notoriously hostility and antagonism may be shown towards what people *are* as well as to what they believe. Thus, although historically the problem of toleration has its origins in religious contexts, and the plea for toleration (in Locke, for example) was a plea for the toleration of different and conflicting beliefs, the modern world has also borne witness to increasing intolerance of what people are. And it is this dimension of the problem on which Michael Ignatieff focuses. He writes: 'the intolerance in which I am interested is directed not at what people believe, but towards who they are, that is, to the totality of those signs (skin colour, religion, language, dietary customs, dress and behaviour) which demarcate them as different.'[6] However, intolerance of belief and intolerance of what people are share an 'irrational' dimension, since both are directed towards things over which the individual has no control. Locke emphasised the irrationality of intolerance in the religious case by noting that belief is not subject to the will. We cannot, he says, choose what to believe and therefore it is futile to deploy the coercive power of the state against people who believe the 'wrong' thing: 'such is the nature of the understanding, that it cannot be compelled to the belief of anything by outward force. Confiscation of estate, imprisonment, torments, nothing of that nature can have any such efficacy as to make men change the inward judgement that they have framed of things.'[7] If this is true of belief, it is yet more true of skin colour and ethnic origin, and therefore we might conclude that here too intolerance has an irrational dimension. Indeed, insofar as arguments against intolerance are grounded in considerations of what it is within the power of the individual to control, intolerance of skin colour or ethnic origin seem even more irrational than intolerance of religious belief.[8]

These reflections on the conditions of toleration help us to understand the centrality of the political, for in a world in which there is hostility between people, and where that hostility is directed towards beliefs or other characteristics which lie outside the power of the individual to control, the question of toleration will become political in two ways. Firstly, it will be a question which arises for those in political power, since they will be in a position to decide how much toleration is to be exercised and in which direction. And although this normally means the majority group, that is not invariably the case, as Garrett Fitzgerald reminds us in his discussion of the case of Northern Ireland. Secondly, the question of whether to tolerate will often be posed in response to the threat of political instability or strife, and this is something of which Christopher Hill reminds us in his discussion of toleration in the seventeenth century. In opposition to those who see the growth of toleration as a manifestation of the increasing powers of reasoned argument, Hill notes the socio-political dimension of the problem, and argues that 'burning heretics was discontinued because . . . it roused too much sympathy for the victims, and so no longer discouraged the others', that 'toleration was a practical necessity if money was to be made through international trade', and that 'by the end of the seventeenth century it had come to be appreciated that market forces were more effective in controlling dissent than erratic state terror.'[9]

Thus, the causes of intolerance are often things which lie outside the power of individuals to control: belief, skin colour, ethnic origin are all potential objects of intolerance, yet they are also things which individuals have little, if any, power to alter. And where the roots of intolerance lie outside reason, we may wonder whether its remedies must also lie outside reason. Where reason cannot operate, we must, it seems, turn to politics.

The remedies for intolerance

What kinds of political remedy are available to counter intolerance? The contributors divide on this question and where Ignatieff, for example, expresses doubts about the desirability of encouraging collective identities, Julia Neuberger and Helena Kennedy both claim that the preservation of such identities is necessary for the growth of toleration. Ignatieff's doubts spring from reflection on the fact that collective identities often gain their power by enabling invidious comparisons to be drawn between members of different groups. It is not simply the case that we affirm our identity through membership of a group; it is also (and often) the case that the group affirms its identity by setting itself against different groups. For Ignatieff, the appropriate response to this problem is to move away from 'adventitious collective identities like race, colour, creed, gender, or sexual orientation'. These are, in the end, minor differences, and if we hope to have a tolerant society we must place faith in the possibility of individuals freeing themselves, one by one, from the 'deadly dynamic' of its narcissism.

By contrast, both Julia Neuberger and Helena Kennedy are more optimistic that the affirmation of group identity will result in a more tolerant society. Although they both emphasise the problems which are inherent in this approach, they nonetheless believe that collective identities are an irreducible part of individual identity and that it is only when group membership is acknowledged and accepted politically that we will be able to move towards a truly tolerant society.

Thus, Kennedy argues that a precondition of becoming an individual is that one's ethnic identity should be recognised:

> a sense of civic identity cannot be forced on people. They must adopt it voluntarily, and this will happen only when they feel that their society respects them and responds to their common needs, including their need for a sense of ethnic identity. That is why it is so important for a government and its ministers to foster an appreciation of diversity in all its forms. Rather than using the language of exclusion, they should be creating the conditions that allow all groups within society to feel a sense of common purpose and mutual respect.[10]

And similarly Neuberger urges members of the established church to 'make space' for members of different religious groups in the corridors of political power.[11]

However, the differences between Ignatieff on the one hand and Kennedy and Neuberger on the other should not be exaggerated. Although they have different evaluations of the prudence of encouraging group identity, this difference is, in part, strategic; for all acknowledge the *de facto* centrality of group identity to individual identity. The crucial question is whether the encouragement of group identity is something which, in an ideal world, will wither away and die. Ignatieff believes that in a liberal utopia, 'adventitious' differences will cease to matter, whereas Kennedy and Neuberger note that, in the world as it is, they do matter and must therefore be acknowledged rather than ignored.

The question of whether we should aspire to a world in which differences matter less is important both politically and conceptually. Michael Ignatieff and Christopher Hill, in their different ways, both urge a movement in the direction of indifference. Ignatieff emphasises the fact that intolerance is frequently provoked by 'minor differences' and he suggests that its remedy is therefore to recognise how minor and unimportant these differences really are. Hill emphasises the historical fact that intolerance wanes when indifference takes its place: in the seventeenth century 'toleration came not because men became wider and nicer, but because circumstances had changed. Toleration comes only when men become indifferent to the issues involved.'[12]

What this suggests is that whereas at the conceptual level toleration is a virtue which requires hostility or disapproval as the ground of its operation, at the political level it might best be cultivated by fostering indifference. Put differently, we might find that a successful political response to intolerance is not one which fosters toleration, but one which renders toleration unnecessary. However, Julia Neuberger casts doubt on this response, partly because she fears that it is one which removes intolerance by the wrong route. To cease to care about the differences which divide us is not to be tolerant. That much is a conceptual truth. But at the more practical level, toleration rooted in indifference runs the risk of misunderstanding its objects. Thus, she argues that:

> one of the reasons why tolerance is difficult in its true sense for many Christians is that they have failed to see what it is that they are being asked to be tolerant of. It is not of a different faith *per se*, though that is part of it. It is of cultural definitions, cultural allegiances that are expressed by religious ritual, as well as profound religious faith.[13]

In short, to become 'tolerant' by becoming indifferent is (or can be) a sign that one is treating as insignificant features of a person's life which are central to his or her own self-understanding and identity.

Thus, the contributors differ about what constitutes an appropriate political response to the problem of intolerance. If, with Ignatieff, we construe the differences which provoke hostility as 'minor differences' and if, with Fitzgerald, we think those differences ought to be transcended by an increased sense of human solidarity, then we will be inclined to envisage a utopia which is largely individualist, and where group identity diminishes in significance. However, if we follow Kennedy and Neuberger in thinking that a secure group identity is a condition for the development of individual identity, then we will envisage a utopia in which people feel secure in their ethnic, religious and other group identities, and where such identities prosper and flourish.

Is there any way of reconciling these two apparently disparate responses to the problem of intolerance in the late twentieth century? What political arrangements, if any, could do justice to the views of both parties? I now turn to these questions and to the proposals advanced both by the contributors to this volume and in political philosophy more generally.

The value of toleration

One way of attempting to reconcile the opposing viewpoints is to be found in the theory of liberal neutrality whose most famous exponent is John Rawls.[14] Rawls takes as given the fact that there are differences between people which give rise to hostility, and he argues that a just political order will be one which, while acknowledging these differences, takes no side in disputes between them. The liberal state will (as far as possible) remain neutral between Christians and Jews, Jews and Sikhs, Sikhs and Muslims, Muslims and atheists. Each group will be allowed to practise its own religion within the liberal state, but the state itself will not endorse any particular religious doctrine. It will simply provide a just arena within which each group can live according to its own tenets and unhindered by others. Allying himself to this Rawlsian solution, Bernard Williams argues that the neutral state 'can be seen as enacting toleration. It expresses toleration's peculiar combination of conviction and acceptance, by finding a home for people's various convictions in groups or communities less than the state, while the acceptance of diversity is located in the structure of the state itself.'[15]

Nonetheless, and as Williams points out, this combination of conviction and acceptance cannot be entirely neutral, for it requires a shared commitment to the political system itself, and to the value it places on showing equal respect to all within an overarching framework of human rights. Furthermore, it requires acknowledgement of the value of individual autonomy, since the emergence of toleration as a distinctive *value* of liberal societies rests, in part, on the claim that people are entitled to lead their own lives in whatever way they think best. We may, at a personal level, deplore those values. Nevertheless, we should tolerate them at the political level precisely because we believe that it is important for people to live in ways which they themselves have endorsed.

This distinction between the values people can appeal to in conducting their own lives and those they can appeal to in justifying the exercise of political power therefore promises a middle way between a recognition of collective identities and an acknowledgement of individuality. Solidarity at the global level is manifested in according human rights to all people independent of race, colour or creed. However, this does not deny the significance of differences which may persist, protected and limited by human rights themselves. On this account it is the recognition of differences, and of their permanence, which enables toleration to be understood as more than a simple expedient in times when political unrest threatens. The Cain and Abel syndrome is averted, not by denying difference, nor yet by becoming indifferent to it, but rather by 'taming' it through the mechanism of the liberal state.

Predictably, however, even this attempt to finesse the problem encounters objections and difficulties. In the first place, and as Bernard Williams points out, there will be some cases in which it simply is not possible for the state to be neutral. Thus, in the debate over abortion, for example, there is no neutral place for the state to occupy: either abortion is legally permitted or it is not, and either way the state will be implicated in supporting one conception of the good over another. Furthermore, and as hinted at above, the state will not even aspire to complete neutrality over absolutely everything. Its commitment to toleration as a value and not simply as a dictate of political prudence springs from the belief that people are autonomous individuals, entitled to equal concern and respect. It will not, therefore, aspire to neutrality with respect to those religious, moral or other beliefs which deny equality or repress the development of autonomy. Toleration has limits, and for liberal neutrality those limits are reached in the encounter with groups who would deny equality and autonomy, or reject the protection afforded by human rights.

These, however, are not the only problems which the liberal state may encounter. In the final contribution to this collection, Alasdair MacIntyre draws attention to a further, and potentially more profound difficulty. His concern echoes and develops that advanced by Julia Neuberger and enables us to see more clearly what exactly is at issue between those who hope for the demise of group difference and those who insist on its permanence. Although MacIntyre endorses many of the conclusions of liberalism, and in particular agrees that the state ought not to impose any conception of the good on those who live under it, he denies that this refusal to impose is a manifestation of neutrality. On the contrary, he argues, the vocabulary of the modern liberal state is the vocabulary of rights and utility, and thus the liberal state, far from being neutral, is committed to certain sorts of value. Furthermore, and in opposition to Williams, MacIntyre does not construe this failure of neutrality as simply a facet of the state's role in encouraging individual autonomy, for 'the state cannot be trusted to promote any worthwhile set of values', including the value of autonomy. In his eyes, then, the alleged neutrality of the liberal state is simply a charade – and a dangerous charade when it takes upon itself a role it can never fulfil, the role of promoting autonomy.

Why is the state untrustworthy in this respect? One major reason has already been foreshadowed in the discussion of other contributions to this collection: namely, that the development of genuine autonomy requires allegiances to smaller groups whose values may be in conflict with the values of the overarching state. MacIntyre writes:

> the values of state and market are not only different from, but on many types of occasion incompatible with, the values of local . . . community. For the former, decision-making is arrived at by a summing of preferences and by a series of trade-offs, in which whose preferences are summed and what is traded off against what depends upon the political and economic bargaining power of the representatives of contending interests. For the latter, a shared understanding of the common good of the relevant type of activity or sets of activities provides a standard independent of preferences and interests, one by reference to which individual preferences and group interests are to be evaluated.[16]

The central thought here is that when the state takes it upon itself to promote autonomy among its citizens, it is also, and thereby, promoting a 'market' understanding of autonomy, but this market understanding is deeply at odds with the values constitutive of many genuine communities and thus the state does not in fact foster autonomy; it fosters a particular, and disputed, conception of autonomy.

The argument is an extension and elaboration of Julia Neuberger's warning that in addressing problems of toleration we must be careful to understand what it is that we are being asked to be tolerant of. 'Solutions' to the problem of toleration which succeed only by distorting the nature of what is tolerated are a deceit. And for this reason MacIntyre arrives at the rather startling conclusion that, in modern politics, toleration is not a virtue at all, and indeed that 'too inclusive a toleration is a vice.'[17]

Conclusion

We began with the story of Cain and Abel, and with consternation at the way in which the modern world combines increasing solidarity at the global level with increasing intolerance at the local level. It seems that as we become more aware of our responsibilities to strangers, we simultaneously become more hostile towards our brothers. Two responses to the Cain and Abel syndrome have been canvassed: the first advocates a move away from adventitious identities like race, colour, creed, gender or sexual orientation. The second urges the acknowledgement and inclusion of those, and other, identities as central features in people's lives. Liberal political theory attempts to attain a *rapprochement* between these two apparently opposing positions by arguing for a state which acknowledges the fact of pluralism as permanent and allows room for different conceptions of the good (different moral and religious views), while at the same time refusing to take any stance itself on which of these conceptions of the good is correct. However, the neutrality of the liberal state can never be complete, for it will have a commitment to certain core values, such as autonomy and equality, and some argue that its commitment to these values threatens to distort the values held by smaller communities within society. When that happens, it is argued, the state cannot be genuinely tolerant: its pretension to toleration is nothing more than a charade.

And so our original problem persists: at the political level, the Cain and Abel syndrome appears to be generated by a tendency to magnify the 'minor differences' which divide people one from another. Yet attempts to increase toleration by emphasising a wider human solidarity run the risk of diminishing and distorting the significance of those collective identities which are (at least arguably) a precondition of people's ability to acknowledge wider solidarity. Modern liberal societies pride themselves on their commitment to toleration as a value, as more than merely a political expedient. What the contributions to this volume suggest is that that commitment may be both more difficult and yet more urgent than is usually recognised.

Notes

1. See below, p. 98.
2. See below, p. 15.
3. J. W. Gough 'The Development of John Locke's Belief in Toleration', in John Horton and Susan Mendus (eds) *John Locke: A Letter Concerning Toleration in Focus*, London, Routledge, 1991, p. 74.
4. See below, p. 46.
5. See below, p. 65.
6. See below, p. 85.
7. Horton and Mendus, *John Locke, p. 18.*
8. Intolerance of skin colour or ethnic origin is also more problematic because it is hard to see how skin colour or ethnic origin can be legitimate objects of disapproval. This difference raises important philosophical points, which are discussed in Susan Mendus, *Toleration and the Limits of Liberalism*, London, Macmillan, 1989.
9. See below, pp. 38, 41.
10. See below, pp. 110–111.
11. See below, p. 130.
12. See below, p. 37.
13. See below, p. 129.
14. John Rawls, *A Theory of Justice*, Oxford, Oxford University Press, 1971, and *Political Liberalism*, Columbia, Columbia University Press, 1993.
15. See below, p. 70.
16. See below, p. 142.
17. See below, p. 153.

Chapter 2

Toleration or solidarity?
Garrett Fitzgerald

Although intolerance is a negative concept it does not follow that toleration is a wholly positive one. The following quotation from a 1927 Edition of a Roman Catholic theology textbook, *Abrégé de Théologie Morale*, illustrates why that is so: 'Evil and error, being nothing, or the negation of being, can have no rights. Civil society can tolerate them for a grave reason, but evil and error can have neither the right nor the freedom to seduce men.' The meaning of 'toleration' may have changed for the better during the years since 1927, but to me at least the word still carries echoes of at best grudging acceptance, and at worst ill-disguised hostility. I therefore propose to discuss, not toleration only, but also human solidarity, and I wish to ask how we can move out, each of us, from our laager to embrace our fellow men as equals.

I use the term 'human solidarity' to mean the solidarity of the human race, because it has to be recognised that there are solidarities that are less than universal, for example solidarities between individuals belonging to a particular group. These partial solidarities are not necessarily components of a wider human solidarity, and they may even be strongly inimical to it, for a partial solidarity is almost always in some degree directed *against* those not included within it, or may indeed derive its strength from a fear of other outside groups. In either event this kind of solidarity can be associated with intolerance rather than tolerance.

During the course of human history there has been a sporadic widening of the sense of solidarity from narrow groups, such as the family or the tribe, to the nation or the state, and in some instances even beyond that. At various points in history some empires have attempted to widen the sense of solidarity to people outside the state which created the empire. In the Roman Empire, for example, there was an attempt to achieve a wider sense of solidarity by extending the concept of Roman citizenship to members of all the races within the empire. Indeed, by the standards of the time, that empire was remarkably successful in this attempt, as may be seen both from the way in which it drew its emperors in later centuries from every part of the empire, and from the way in which Roman citizenship and Roman law took permanent root throughout its territory. Two thousand years later the Romance languages of Western Europe, and even of Romania, and the civil law of much of Western Europe, testify to the success of this far-sighted Roman policy.

In recent times, too, certain empires have aspired in some degree to a similar extension of solidarity – although not with the same willingness as the Roman Empire to allow leadership to be undertaken by people of races other than the founding race.

Moreover, in the latter part of this century a conscious attempt has been made to achieve, through the creation of the European Community, a limited but highly significant extension of solidarity amongst the peoples of Western Europe. Here, of course, the concept of solidarity has no imperial connotations and the intention has been to create a new and wider sense of solidarity inclusive of, but not in place of, the sense of solidarity of the peoples of the states taking part in it. However, it has to be recognised that even in the case of the European Community, while it has certainly not built or encouraged intolerance of others outside its own area, it has derived much of its initial motivation from a combination of fear of the Soviet Union and concern about commercial competition from the United States, and later from Japan, as well, perhaps, as concern about a loss of European identity in the face of pervasive American mass culture.

The most interesting and encouraging feature of this century, however, has been the emergence of an embryonic wider sense of *human solidarity*. In a way that few could have thought possible, and many would not even have wished to contemplate sixty years ago, a growing proportion of the human race has today *some* sense of solidarity with people and peoples in other lands, and a further fraction of the human race at least pays lip service to this concept.

By contrast let us recall that, in 1927, when this edition of my theology book was published, hundreds of millions of people over quite a large part of the earth's surface were inhabitants of colonial empires, and the peoples of the colonial powers in question took it for granted that a colonist/subject relationship was a quite normal and appropriate one. Many of them took equally for granted the propriety of a transfer of resources from colonised to coloniser, even though some historians now tell us that such transfers were in fact rarer and less ample than people then assumed. Of course there are still *some* people in Europe who feel this way, but they are today the exceptions. A far greater number of people in Europe and elsewhere in the world now hold a diametrically opposite view, viz. that the peoples of richer countries, such as those of Europe and other developed parts of the world, have a duty to transfer some of their current resources annually to poorer peoples. Exploitation as an acceptable norm of behaviour has thus been replaced by solidarity. During a period in which religion itself has lost much ground, the gospel concept of every man being one's neighbour has belatedly come to be quite widely accepted.

Of course, this thesis needs to be heavily qualified. The new sense of solidarity with other peoples remains notably imperfect, and even where it has taken hold, its grip is loose. The sense of duty that many have come to feel towards poorer neighbours elsewhere in the world is still today relatively lightly discharged. Judging by the statistics for development aid, the general conscience of the peoples of developed countries is satisfied with the transfer annually of a pittance of one-three-hundredth part of their current resources to poorer peoples, many of whom have material living standards less than one-twentieth of those of the donor countries, and a significant proportion of whom at any given time are hungry or even starving.

Nevertheless, whatever the adequacy of its practical expression, the fact that the *concept* of international solidarity is now widely accepted is immensely significant. This acceptance reflects one of the most extraordinary transformations in human attitudes that has occurred in history, and it is all the more remarkable for having been scarcely remarked by those who have lived through and been party to it. What this reflects is a sense of the unity of the human race which was certainly foreshadowed by the teaching of Christ two thousand years ago, and to which Christians have always given religious assent, but which until this century had not become part of secular thought or a motivating force in the actions of states.

The emergence of a sense of human solidarity in the present century is probably the product of a number of different factors. The most obvious, perhaps, is the way in which the world has become technologically united during the second half of this century to such an extent that it is possible to fly around the world in a couple of days at the cost of the equivalent of several weeks' pay for an industrial worker in a developed country. Television, above all, has given a sense of immediacy to global human contact. Science and technology may well have contributed to this development in another way also, by enlarging human horizons through the exploration of space, and by discovering the immensity of the expanding universe, of which this planet is such a tiny and insignificant element. To someone whose horizons are bounded by the confines of his own village or region or even state, the rest of the world and its people may seem threatening, but someone who is even slightly aware of the precarious isolation of the human race on this small planet can equally come to feel a real sense of solidarity with his fellow planetarians. Indeed, as people become increasingly aware of the delicate environmental balance of this planet, which may be dangerously disturbed either by cutting down its tropical forests or even by using aerosols which weaken the ozone layer that protects us from ultra-violet rays, a sense of the solidarity not merely of man with man, but of man with the environment in which man lives, has begun to emerge.

It may well be that as this dramatic, and in some respects horrific, century moves towards its close, an emerging sense of the common interest of the human race may be starting to have a profound effect upon our politics. The ability of the two great superpowers to see each other as evil empires threatening each other's existence is now in the process of being undermined by the almost unwilling growth of a sense on the part of the peoples of both these great states that as part of a world community they have a common interest transcending their hitherto deeply felt differences. Just as in the post-war period the countries of Western Europe made a sudden and profound mental adjustment, as a result of which war between them became as unthinkable as it was a regularly recurring feature up to the middle of this century, so also an analogous process has emerged between Russia and the United States following the collapse of the Communist system.

Nonetheless, many will point out that the world we live in is full of the most appalling violence inflicted by men and women on each other; and since the last world war there has been an apparently endless stream of regional conflicts that have cost the lives of tens of millions of people. How then can one take what many would think to be an optimistic view of the future of the human race? The view I have been putting forward would certainly be an optimistic one were it to be presented as a complete picture of where the human race now stands, but so far I have been deliberately dwelling on one aspect only of the human condition in the second half of this century – the first tenuous and tender shoots of human solidarity to appear on a global scale.

There is, of course, another side to the picture, and a very negative one. For at the same time as this wider vision of the human condition has been tentatively emerging, the very technology which has contributed in some degree to its development has, at another level, provided the means by which, in regional conflicts or civil wars, people have become able to kill each other on a vastly greater scale than was possible in the past. The development of more powerful and much cheaper weapons has helped the terrorist, the guerilla, and those prepared to engage in genocide, and the scale of potential profits from the sale of weapons by competing suppliers has given an additional incentive to supply arms on a larger scale, and in relatively balanced quantities, to both sides in any quarrel. The result has been that the lethal process of mutual extermination can be carried on at far more cost to human life, and can be sustained for a much longer period, than might have been possible in the past.

This helps to explain why these regional and internal conflicts have been so lethal, and in many cases so long-lasting. But why have there been so many of them in this period? Some have roots deep in the past, reflecting the survival in a small geographical space of separate identities derived from long-past conflicts. This has been true of Cyprus and of Northern Ireland, for example. Most, however, are either the products of a process of colonisation and decolonisation (for example, South Africa, Mozambique, Sudan, Pakistan, India, Chad), or derive from the Cold War (for example, Korea, Vietnam, Kampuchea, Angola). And there is yet another group comprising, for example, Salvador and Nicaragua, and perhaps Colombia, where the conflict is fundamentally between an oligarchy of landowners and peasants. Finally there is the group of conflicts in the Middle East: Israel and her Arab neighbours, Iran and Iraq, and the internal conflict that racked the Lebanon for a decade and a half.

While it is dangerous to generalise, I shall take the risk of remarking that both the Cold War regional conflicts and a number of the post-colonial conflicts seem to be specific to the second half of the twentieth century, and the Latin American conflicts seem also to be the tail-end of a process of democratisation in particularly anachronistic regimes whose roots lie back in the sixteenth century. In other words, it is possible that as we move towards and into the twenty-first century, the *number* of major regional or internecine conflicts of this type in the world may diminish as the residual consequences of colonisation and the Cold War resolve themselves.

Nevertheless, we are very far from the stage at which we can visualise a peaceful world in the next century, and there is now the added risk of nuclear conflict deriving from the proliferation of nuclear weapons in areas of regional conflict such as Israel, India and Pakistan, and the threat of such a development in some of the countries that aspire to nuclear armament capacity. This proliferation owes much to the venality or stupidity of one or more of the major nuclear powers. The nuclear threat in the twenty-first century seems much more likely to come from this source than from a conflict between the major powers. Although not all will agree with me, I feel that it may be easier for the rulers and peoples of great powers to develop a sense of human solidarity that can transcend their differences and conflicts than it is for people embedded in local conflict situations to raise *their* sights to broader horizons. Countries like the

United States and Russia, which are engaged in space exploration, both competitive and co-operative, may, for example, find it easier to arrive at a sense of sharing an interest in a common destiny than Greeks and Turks in Cyprus, or Israelis and Arabs in Palestine, especially as the smaller the land space in which people with different identities seek to assert themselves, the more intense the conflict between them.

It is not, therefore, really surprising that the growth of a certain sense of human solidarity at one level should have been accompanied by the persistence of intolerance at another level. Intolerance, moreover, is often a function of relationships between distinct communities occupying the same geographical space, or at any rate occupying interlocking and intersecting areas within a geographic space. Animosity can, and very often does, exist between peoples in different and often contiguous geographical areas, but this is not quite the same thing as intolerance. Moreover, there is evidence that animosities between neighbours *can* evaporate (or at any rate be contained within a civilised relationship), much more easily than intolerance can be eradicated. For intolerance is often a function of fear, and fear of a threat from within often runs even deeper than fear of a threat from without.

The fear in question may appear irrational to those who live at a comfortable distance, but that does not alter the fact that the fear is real, even if the source of the fear may be deemed by others to be unreal. In fact, this difference in perception about the reality of fear can itself give rise to what might be described as a second dimension of intolerance, namely the intolerance of intolerance. Thus, for example, many people are unsympathetic to, even intolerant of, Unionists in Northern Ireland because they see many Unionists as themselves intolerant, and do not understand the fears that have brought this about. This lack of sympathy may in turn have reinforced Unionist intolerance which derives not only from fear but from a sense of isolation, to which the negative attitudes of others towards them may contribute. Indeed it may even be the case that an easing of international tensions and a perceptible growth of human solidarity may aggravate the problems of intolerance in mixed communities, where two groups each appear as a threat to the other but where the sense of isolation that one or both groups may feel can be intensified if the world seems to be passing them by.

Something of this has been visible, I believe, in Northern Ireland also, because the growth of religious tolerance in Britain has deprived many Northern Ireland Protestants of the sense they used to have of being part of a wider group of what might be described as active British Protestantism. And it may well be that something of the same phenomenon can be identified as having occurred over the last couple of decades amongst part of the Northern Ireland Catholic community. This is particularly true in West Belfast where the isolated Catholic population have seen the Republic moving, even if fitfully, towards becoming a tolerant, pluralist society.

At the same time, and in Britain itself, the waning of religious intolerance has clearly been accompanied by an intensification of racial intolerance in those areas which were previously racially homogeneous, but which during the post-war period have become racially mixed. It is worth adding perhaps that in confrontation situations of the kind to which I have been referring, intolerance rarely remains entirely one-sided. The fear that induces intolerance will often take the form of concrete actions directed against the feared community, and that action may in turn induce fear, and then intolerance, on the part of the feared community itself.

However, it is worth noting that toleration and intolerance are primarily attitudes of a dominant rather than a subordinate group, for to 'tolerate' something one must be in a dominant or superior position in the first instance. Being dominant, however, is not the same as being in the majority, and where a dominant community is numerically in the minority, its fears will be that much more intense because of the precarious nature of its hold on power in the face of what may be seen as a hostile majority. That, in fact, has been characteristic of the situation in Northern Ireland, but the problem is obscured precisely because Unionists are a majority *within* Northern Ireland, which was permitted, in 1921, to opt out of the newly established Dominion of the Irish Free State. Despite this division, and the fact that objectively there is little prospect of this division of the island disappearing in the foreseeable future, the Unionist majority within that area has remained psychologically conditioned by its position as a minority in the island of Ireland as a whole. Paradoxically, and at the deepest psychological level, it is the Unionists rather than the Nationalists who have never accepted the reality and enduring quality of the division of the island. It is *they*, therefore, who have the fears normally associated in modern states with a minority rather than a majority position.

Indeed, the intensity of the Northern Ireland problem owes a good deal to the paradox that Unionists, with the kinds of fear that normally one associates with a threatened and beleaguered minority, were placed in a local majority position by the division of the island through the Anglo-Irish Treaty. In that situation they were tempted to seek to safeguard, by exceptional and, in part at least, discriminatory measures, their locally dominant position against what they perceived as a threat to that position from a Nationalist majority in the island of Ireland as a whole.

The powder-keg situation which exploded in 1969 was created by the failure of British governments, in both the pre- and post-war periods, to exercise their sovereignty in Northern Ireland in an even-handed way, and to restrain the unacceptable policies embarked on by Unionist governments. The record, as disclosed by Home Office papers published for the period from 1922 onwards, is a depressing one. The inability of other departments of state, such as the Dominions Office and the Foreign Office, to challenge effectively the Home Office policy of inaction reflected the general inability of successive British governments until very recent times to pursue a coherent Irish policy, except for brief periods when the full attention of a government has been temporarily directed towards the problems of Ireland.

The best way to tackle any evil, whether it be intolerance or terrorism, is to seek to eradicate, (or in many cases less ambitiously, but perhaps more appropriately), to mitigate its causes. Where the problem of intolerance arises because of the co-existence of two distinct communities in the same geographical area, eradication of the cause of intolerance may not be practicable in the short or medium run without a resettlement of populations, which is unacceptable in a modern society, and which in any event would be likely to give rise to fresh and perhaps even more explosive grievances amongst the dispossessed. We have seen something of the kind happen in Palestine, and the tragic consequences there are not to be explained solely, as some in Israel contend, in terms of a failure to resettle the dispossessed populations, who were left in refugee camps. In Northern Ireland itself in the early 1970s there was in fact a forced resettlement of a large proportion of the population of Belfast, when 85,000 Nationalists were intimidated from their homes in mixed areas and forced to resettle in the Nationalist ghetto areas, which in turn expanded their boundaries marginally at the expense of a similar forced migration by some 15,000 Unionists. The bitter consequences of this forced population transfer offer little encouragement to the pursuit of such a policy of resettlement as a solution to the Northern Ireland problem. That being the case, efforts have had to be concentrated – with considerable success in the recent past – on mitigating rather than eradicating the causes of intolerance, and on bridging the gulf between the two communities.

It has always seemed to me that the Irish state had a potentially significant role to play in this process, for Unionists' fears of being absorbed into an all-Ireland state, in which they believe their identities would be threatened, are in part at least a function of past irredentist claims by politicians in the Republic. The recent substitution of unambiguous assurances, backed by 95 per cent of the people of the Republic in a referendum, that unification of the island can and should come about *only* with the consent of a majority in Northern Ireland, has been a crucially important, and in my view long overdue, step towards reducing the fear that has lain behind Unionist intolerance in Northern Ireland. However, in the longer term, the objective must be something more than a mitigation of the causes of intolerance. A bridge has to be built between the two communities involved, and this will require an imaginative leap by each side. Each side must seek to understand, and to show understanding of, the other's fears.

However it is not reasonable to expect those most immediately involved to initiate this process. People with a leadership role have to take the initiative and responsibility, and a particular duty has devolved on political leaders and church leaders. Political leaders have had to be prepared to transcend the interests of their own community in a committed and conscientious way, and have had to show some capacity to understand and empathise with the other community. This has carried political risks, but a failure to take risks of this kind has in the past made political activity in the area of intercommunity relations ineffective and indeed counterproductive. This risk-taking must, of course, be well judged, otherwise the capacity to lead one's own community may be eroded and destroyed. Moreover, church leaders bear at least as much responsibility as political leaders, for they are not subject to the same risks as elected politicians. Perhaps this is too sweeping. Not all churches provide security of tenure for their ministers, but most do, and security of tenure carries with it a correlative obligation to bear witness to the truth.

Let me give some examples, involving my own church, of how it seems to me that church leaders could contribute to an easing of tensions by reviewing traditional attitudes. For several decades I have argued that in the Irish case there should be a review of the Roman Catholic requirement that a commitment be given by the Catholic parties to bring up as Catholics the children of a contemplated mixed marriage. The reason I have argued for review is that the requirement had a quite dramatic effect on the number of Protestants in the Republic over the first two generations of the state. During that period one quarter of Protestants married Catholics in each generation, and the resultant reduction in the Protestant population of the Republic intensified Northern Protestant fears of Catholicism by leading to a mistaken belief that the decline in the number of Protestants in the Republic must in some way be due to economic discrimination, which Protestants in the North fear might apply to them in a unified Ireland. The reality is in fact quite different, for Protestants in the Republic, because of their higher average economic status since the last War consistently experienced below-average emigration and 40 per cent of them have higher-level employment – in management, administration and the professions, as against 20 per cent of the Catholic population. Nonetheless, I do not seem to have succeeded in convincing the institutional church, either in Rome or in Ireland, that this consideration should even be taken into account, and I regard this apparent unwillingness even to bring the issue into the balance as one which shows a lack of leadership in a situation of inter-community tension.

Again in relation to mixed schooling, the institutional Catholic Church in Ireland has consistently refused to accept that separate schooling *could* be a factor in maintaining or reinforcing community tensions. Whenever this point is made, churchmen respond by saying that separate schooling is not the *cause* of community tension, and they insist on ignoring the fact that in public opinion polls two-thirds of the Catholic population have consistently stated their preference for mixed education. The unwillingness of the Catholic Church leaders to address this question on its merits again reflects, I believe, a lack of leadership.

A third example is the powerful and, as it turned out in the 1986 Referendum (but not in that of 1995), effective opposition of the institutional Catholic Church in Ireland to the introduction of a highly restrictive form of civil divorce. This opposition manifested itself only two years after the church's official spokesman had proclaimed to the New Ireland Forum that in the event of Irish reunification the Catholic Church would defend most vigorously the civil rights of Northern Protestants – including, it was conveyed, their right to civil divorce. These two positions may be intellectually reconcilable, but not, I believe, in a manner that would convince an average Northern Protestant, prone for reasons of historical conditioning to be suspicious of institutional Catholicism, to liberate himself or herself from such prejudices. And given the lethal consequences for Catholics of Protestant prejudice (exemplified by the many hundreds of random murders of Catholics in the last thirty years), the unwillingness of the institutional Catholic Church to consider whether a modification of attitudes on issues such as these might contribute even a little towards easing the lethal sectarian tensions that threaten Catholic lives is, I feel, open to some questioning.

Lest it be felt that my criticisms are directed only against my own church, I should perhaps add that there are virtually no Roman Catholic equivalents to the anti-Catholic rabble-rousing sermonising of Free Presbyterian Ministers, nor are there more than a tiny handful of Catholic priests whose political involvement could in any way compare with the massive participation of Protestant clergy in the activities of the overtly anti-Catholic Orange Order and its associated bodies. In the light of this record, on both sides, and despite the frequent joint and separate condemnation of violence by Catholic and Protestant churchmen, the record of the churches in Northern Ireland in tackling the *roots* of sectarianism, intolerance and violence is not, I feel, a distinguished one, although there have been some notable and courageous exceptions on both sides.

This rather prolonged excursion into the possible, but not yet actual, role of churches as well as politicians in Ireland in tackling the canker of intolerance may, I am afraid, have distracted attention away from my main theme. This, I have often found, is a danger whenever one illustrates one's theoretical points with examples – but if one remains at the theoretical level without relating one's thesis to life, the point being made is often lost for want of illustration. Better to risk the former fate than the latter!

Let me, however, remind you again of my main theme. There is a striking and tragic contrast between the movement towards human solidarity at the global level and the apparent entrenchment of intolerance at the level of differentiated communities sharing a small geographical space. The gap between the two levels will eventually be bridged, and those of us who may have any role to play in bridging it have a duty to do everything in our power to hasten the reconciliation of such divided communities. So have those who are involved with, or have power to influence, regional wars. Unless tackled with imagination by religious as well as political leaders, these areas of human conflict may remain potent sources of tragedy and misery, perhaps long after the threat of conflict between world powers has receded, and perhaps even ended.

Chapter 3

Toleration in seventeenth-century England: theory and practice
Christopher Hill

Historians of toleration usually talk about *theories* of toleration, and depict a gradual victory of reason and common sense over irrational prejudice. This movement, slowly broadening down, is sometimes interrupted by thinkers who 'fail to see the logic of their own arguments', as when the very tolerant Milton and Locke refused to extend religious toleration to Roman Catholics. The reason for this refusal was *not* that they failed to understand their own arguments. It is twentieth-century commentators who fail to understand what Milton and Locke were talking about.

I want to suggest that the evolution of toleration was not a smooth intellectual process, proceeding from argument to argument until all were convinced. If we look at the struggle for toleration on the ground, so to speak, taking account of the attitudes of heretics demanding freedom of worship and of those who resisted those demands, the picture looks rather different. Historically, toleration is a practice rather than a theory.

However, I don't want to suggest that what the books say about progress is not absolutely right. We cannot too often remind ourselves that English men and women were being burnt alive for their religious beliefs as late as 1612, and that Archbishop Neile of York, who participated in sentencing the last victims, said in 1639 that he thought it would be a good thing to revive the practice. Burning heretics had done the church a great deal of good, he said nostalgically – as he no doubt thought the flogging, ear-slitting and branding which Archbishop Laud favoured had done. But Neile was too late: the Revolution of the 1640s prevented any revival of burning for heresy (though women continued to be burnt for husband-murder well into the eighteenth century: men were hanged for killing their wives). But when bishops came back with the King in 1660, Thomas Hobbes was afraid they would try to burn him. I am sure Hobbes was right in thinking that some bishops would have liked to burn him. But it really was too late, though men continued to be hanged for blasphemy and rejecting the Trinity as late as the 1690s.

I shall talk about seventeenth-century people whom I know best – Bunyan and the early Quakers, though I am sure my points could be made on the basis of any number of other examples. Bunyan first faced intolerance in 1660, when he was thirty-two years old. He was twelve years old when in 1640 the traditional Church of England collapsed, and with it the censorship which the Church had controlled. For the next twenty years men and women were no longer legally obliged to attend their parish church every Sunday and listen to the ministrations of a clergyman in whose selection they had had no say, and whose theology and personality they might detest. Frustrated sectaries heckled persons, seized pulpits from their legal occupants and preached themselves. No one could stop laymen – and indeed women – from preaching. All over the country congregations sprang up which ran their own affairs democratically just as they wished. Many elected a so-called 'mechanic preacher', an artisan (unordained, of course) who worked with his hands six days a week and took the chair at a discussion group on the seventh day. The tinker Bunyan was a mechanic preacher. Men and women were free to *choose* between several places of worship, even to choose none at all. It was a quite unique experience.

The press was free after 1640, and open to people who could not possibly have got into print earlier. Bunyan in the late fifties enjoyed (the right word, I think) a fierce and scurrilous theological con-troversy with early Quakers. But in 1660 all that changed. Bishops came back with Charles II. Once more all were deemed to be members of the Church of England, liable to be fined if they did not attend its services every Sunday. They had to pay tithes and to accept the discipline of church courts. Religious meetings other than those of the national church were again illegal. Laymen were of course forbidden to preach, as were women. JPs from the gentry who had been panic-stricken by the upheavals of the forties and fifties could now take savage revenge against those whom they regarded as their enemies.

At the restoration Bunyan was arrested, charged with illegal preaching to illegal conventicles. He was told he must either give an undertaking never to preach again, or go to jail indefinitely. Bunyan believed he had been called by God to preach, and that he could not give it up. His judges replied that his vocation was that of a tinker, not a preacher. He was a layman, unordained, and uneducated in the sense that he had not been to a university or even (so far as we know) to a grammar school. A tinker indeed was socially the lowest of the low. So they sent Bunyan to prison, where he remained for twelve years. In most cases this would have been a death sentence in view of the horribly insanitary condition of English prisons; but Bunyan, like George Fox, was exceptionally tough, morally and physically. He survived.

This, the books tell us, is an example of religious persecution, and so it was. But let us look at it on the ground. Bunyan's spell in prison was longer than that meted out to anyone at the restoration who was not a regicide or an active revolutionary leader. Bunyan was no political leader; politics were by no means his main concern. Why, then, was he singled out for such severe treatment by the Bedfordshire justices?

A sermon by Bunyan which was printed in 1659 may give us a clue.[1] It was on the parable of Dives and Lazarus, the rich man who goes to hell whilst the 'poor scabbed hedge-creep' Lazarus, whom Dives used to spurn as he lay at his gate begging for alms, went to heaven. However, Dives was permitted to see Lazarus in heaven. He begged that Lazarus might be allowed to dip his finger in cold water and moisten Dives's lips, but it was too late. Bunyan, a regular hell-fire preacher, used this parable to put the fear of hell into rich men. Throughout his writings Bunyan was always passionately on the side of the poor, fiercely hostile to the rich. In *The Pilgrim's Progress* every one of the bad characters is invariably, and obsessively, described as a lady or a gentleman, except when they are lords. 'The poor,' Bunyan wrote later, 'because they are poor, are not capable of sinning against God as the rich man does.' 'More servants than masters . . . more tenants than landlords, will inherit the kingdom of heaven'.[2] Christ rejects 'the great ones that were the grandees of the world', preferring 'hedge-creepers and highwaymen'. 'God's little ones' 'are not gentlemen . . . cannot, with Pontius Pilate, speak Hebrew, Greek and Latin'. In his sermon on Dives and Lazarus Bunyan seems almost to have some individuals in mind when he describes how 'the great ones of the world will go strutting up and down the streets'. 'They will build houses for their dogs, when the saints must be glad to wander and lodge in dens and caves of the earth.'[3] These phrases, which come from the one sermon of Bunyan's that had so far been printed, are reminiscent of the dreamer of *The Pilgrim's Progress*, and they prompt us to ask what he said in all his other sensationally popular sermons. Were they even more offensive? Were the characters denounced in them even more recognisable?

The Bedfordshire gentry described Bunyan as 'a pestilential fellow', the worst in the county. A pamphleteer described him as 'a turbulent spirit', whose 'licentious and destructive principles' would lead to the 'subversion of all government'. 'Natural brute beasts' like Bunyan, said the reverend writer of these remarks, 'should be taken and destroyed.'[4] He described himself as a spokesman of 'the moderate divines', and he was soon to become a bishop. One wonders about the less moderate.

The Bedfordshire gentry knew a lot about Bunyan. They did not think of him just as a godly nonconformist preacher. He had been a soldier in the army which had defeated Charles I. The congregation of which he was a leading member had been active in politics in the 1650s, as had been most of the separatist congregations. It applauded the army's expulsion of the Rump of the Long Parliament in 1643, and recommended suitable persons to sit in the 'Barebones Parliament' which the army leaders then set up. The congregation urged Oliver Cromwell not to accept the crown when Parliament offered it to him in 1657. When he refused it they set aside a day of thanks to

God. They opposed the restoration of Charles II, after which they never again recorded any discussions on politics. That was what the restoration had been about.

The Bedfordshire gentry wanted to silence Bunyan. If he had agreed to silence himself, he would have gone free. Instead he spent twelve years in jail, at the cost of who knows what suffering to his wife and five children, one of them blind. His second wife's first child died when she was 'dismayed at the news of her husband's arrest'. When he was ultimately released Bunyan at once started breaking the law again. Most of the forty-odd books which he published between his arrest and his death in 1688 were printed illegally, without licence. His printers were almost invariably seditious radicals, who spent most of their time in and out of prison, were pilloried, and suffered heavy fines, fees and damages. One of them fought for Monmouth in his rebellion of 1685; others went into exile. When a printer was asked why he had not licensed one of Bunyan's books before publication, as the law required, he replied simply 'I knew I shouldn't get a licence for Bunyan.' His reputation had spread from Bedfordshire to London, so though Bunyan was certainly not a political figure, he had politics forced upon him by the policies of post-restoration governments and JPs. The authorities were right to be worried about the dangers of unrest after 1660. There were many plots for armed revolt in the years 1660–3, in some of which Bunyan's friends were involved. They culminated in the Yorkshire rising of 1663. The government tended to regard any illegal meeting as potentially seditious: how could they distinguish?

So when Bunyan faced the Bedfordshire justices in 1661 he thought he was refusing to give up his God-given vocation of preaching; they thought he was a dangerous agitator who was stirring up class hostility in the very delicate situation of post-restoration England, just recovering from a revolution in which the revolutionaries had spoken on behalf of the poor, as Bunyan did. The issues are not clear-cut, not pure, for two quite different politico-religious systems of values were in conflict. The Bedfordshire gentry believed it to be their duty to prevent disorder, and in particular to prevent any revival of the revolutionary activities of the forties and fifties. Bunyan's motives were religious, not political, not revolutionary. Nonetheless, they led him to take actions which the Bedfordshire justices could not but regard as seditious. They were enforcing the laws of the land. The case of Bunyan therefore raises sharply a question which is still relevant today, the question of whether resistance to the law is ever legitimate when it seems to be dictated by sincere conscientious beliefs (though seventeenth-century laws were not passed by democratically elected Parliaments). Bunyan, so far as we know, took no part in seditious conspiracy, but many of his close associates did. For Bunyan and his like their congregations were defensive units of freedom and solidarity in which they could continue the sort of unhampered worship and discussions to which they had become accustomed in the forties and fifties.

Quakers faced similar problems. We think of Quakers as pacifists, people who take no part in politics. That is true of eighteenth-century and later Quakers, but it was not true of Quakers in the 1650s and early 1660s. Many Quakers had fought in the Parliamentarian armies against Charles I, and did not resign from the army when they were convinced. They protested when they were dismissed because of their refusal to take oaths and because their egalitarian principles, as one general put it, were 'inconsistent with the discipline of an army'. Many rejoined the army in 1659–60 in the hope of preventing a restoration of monarchy.

Most of the leading Quakers in the 1650s (and not only Quakers) expected the Second Coming of Jesus Christ and the millennium in the immediate future. Quakers inherited many of the principles of Levellers, Diggers and Ranters, the radical wing of the Parliamentarians, all of whom had been suppressed between 1649 and 1651. (The first appearance of Quakers dates from 1652–3.) Like Bunyan, Quakers attacked the rich and spoke up for the poor. 'O ye great men and rich men of the earth,' Fox cried in 1653, 'weep and howl, for your misery is coming.'[5] Quakers refused to remove their hats in the presence of social superiors or magistrates, and they used the familiar 'thou' rather than the deferential 'you' when speaking to their betters. These were old radical habits. Quakers attacked lawyers, and wished to abolish them: they wanted drastic reformation of the law on behalf of the poor. Most upsetting was their habit of making public symbolic demonstrations. It was odd when Fox walked through Lichfield, naked except for a loincloth round his middle for decency's sake, shouting 'Woe to the bloody city of Lichfield!'; it was rather more than odd when Mary Todd 'pulled up all her clothes above her middle, exposing her nakedness to all', crying 'welcome the resurrection'. Similarly with public burnings of the Bible, by others as well as Quakers, because it was not the Word of God, because it deceived people.

Quakers refused to pay tithes, and incited others to refuse. Tithes went to support a clergyman in every parish in the country: Milton and many others thought that religious freedom was impossible without their abolition, which would have amounted to disestablishment of the state church, but conservatives saw a national church as essential to thought control. Governments wanted appointed (not elected) interpreters of the Bible in every parish, men who had been educated at Oxford or Cambridge, and so would not have a dangerous idea in their heads.

In the sudden unaccustomed freedom, discussion and speculation on all sorts of subjects hitherto taboo had been possible. Democracy, communism, free love, the desirability of church marriage, comparative religion, the truth and reliability of the Bible – all these had been the subject of eager argument. The Quaker Samuel Fisher published a large scholarly tome showing that the Bible was so internally inconsistent and self-contradictory that it could not be the Word of God.[6] Ranters argued that 'sin' had been invented by the ruling class to keep the lower orders down, and that you could sleep with anyone your conscience said you might. The young Bunyan liked that, 'I being a young man and my nature at its prime'. One Ranter claimed that God had told him to break all the Ten Commandments except 'Thou shalt do no murder'. And he wondered whether that was still to come. Quakers participated actively in all these discussions, often on the radical side. They were often confused with Ranters, and indeed many Ranters after their suppression in 1650–1 became Quakers.

Quakers used extremely bellicose Biblical language, which may have been intended allegorically; but what would nervous

contemporaries have thought? Edward Burrough, political spokesman for the Quakers, cried in 1655, 'Let not your eye pity nor
your hand spare, but wound the lofty and tread under foot the
honourable of the earth.' Howgil, another leading Quaker, said a
year later, 'spare none, neither old nor young; kill, cut off, destroy,
bathe your sword in the blood of Amalek'. When Christ comes,
Burrough declared in 1657, 'all that would not that Christ should
reign, slay them before him'. Fox stated that 'the saints of the most
high God are coming to break [his enemies] in pieces'. 'The saints
shall judge the world . . . whereof I am one.' 'A day of slaughter is
coming to you who have made war against the Lamb and against
the saints . . . The sword cannot escape, and it shall be upon you
before long.'[7]

Fox wrote a tract specially for members of the Army, urging them
to 'see that you know a soldier's place . . . and that ye be soldiers
qualified'. Fox frequently urged Cromwell and the army to pursue an
aggressive European crusade against popery. 'Let they soldiers go
forth', he told the Protector in January 1658, 'that thou may rock
nations as a cradle.' 'Had you been faithful to the power of the Lord,'
he complained to the army the following year, 'you had gone into
the midst of Spain . . . gone over them as the wind, and knocked at
Rome's gates before now, and trampled deceit and tyrants under.' In
1659 he told 'soldiers and true officers . . . if ever you . . . come again
into the power of God which hath been lost, never set up your
standard till you come to Rome.'[8]

The Quakers had enjoyed the protection of the radical New
Model Army against conservative JPs and town magistrates. Colonel
Scroops, commander of the garrison of Bristol, declared in 1654 of
Quakers 'if the magistrates did put them in prison one day, he would
put them out the next'. When the garrison was moved from Bristol,
Quakers had a much tougher time. In 1659–60, as the restoration of
monarchy appeared to be looming, Quakers offered their support to
the republican government and the army in order to keep out
Charles II. 'Those who desired an earthly king', Fox snorted, were
'traitors against Christ'. 'True Christians will have no king but
Christ.' Quakers rejoined the army, raised troops, accepted office
as JPs. Some think that panic fear of Quakers and their subversive

intentions did much to expedite the restoration of monarchy. There was much talk of 'arming the Quakers'. Some thought 'the whole Army would be reduced to follow' the Quakers.

Only after the restoration, and after a revolt in London by Desperate Fifth Monarchists which terrorised London for days, was the Quaker peace principle announced, in January 1661. Their proclamation of pacifism was an attempt to distinguish Quakers from Fifth Monarchists and other still belligerent sectaries. In the long run the peace principle established the Quakers as a community who abjured 'the carnal sword' and withdrew from political activity. It was a recognition that the millennium was not coming in England in the near future, that the saints were not going to rule, and ultimately that Christ's kingdom was not of this world. This was a great reversal. But it took time for the fact to be accepted.

Many Quakers in 1661 regarded the peace principle and the discipline which was necessary to enforce it as a betrayal of Quaker principles. There were many splits, for example John Perrot and his followers, and the Story–Wilkinson separation. Many Quakers took part in the Yorkshire rising of 1663, and as late as 1685 at least twelve Quakers joined Monmouth's rebellion, of whom three were executed. For these reasons conservatives were slow to accept the genuineness of Quaker pacifism and so the possibility of extending toleration to them. Quakers continued to refuse payment of tithes with greater courage and determination than other sects. Their rejection of oaths was another sticking point: refusal to take the oath of loyalty to the restored monarchy entailed a jail sentence and was presumptive evidence of disloyalty. Not until 1696 was the genuineness of Quaker principled objection to oaths recognised, and they were allowed to affirm.

I am not suggesting it was right to persecute Quakers or Bunyan – far from it. But it was not a simple straightforward issue of 'religious freedom', in which all the reasons are on one side. Extreme language and provocative gestures were natural reactions to frustration: Quakers (and others) felt that they had to make a scene in order to get a hearing. What I am suggesting is that in the seventeenth century, when state and church were one – perhaps in other societies where party and state are one – toleration is a *political* issue, inseparable from politico-social questions which historians of toleration sometimes overlook.

It is not easy for us to understand why many sincere defenders of religious toleration like Milton and (later) Locke drew the line at toleration for Roman Catholics. They were prepared to grant freedom to Ranters, to Quakers who disrupted other people's church services, to fight Monarchists who believed in establishing the rule of the saints, by force if necessary. Historians of toleration often say that Milton and Locke failed to understand the logic of their own arguments. That is, frankly, just silly. They were highly intelligent men. They had what they (and many others) believed to be good reasons for refusing toleration to papists. We may not accept these arguments; but we must try to understand them. Men felt that they were involved in a life-and-death struggle between Protestantism and the forces of Antichrist, that England's national independence and the future of humanity were at stake. It was not possible, such men thought, to extend freedom of organisation to Catholics, to the adherents of Antichrist – the pope and his followers. There could be no compromise with papists who had tried to subordinate England to Spain in Bloody Mary's reign, had organised the Spanish Armada, Guy Fawkes's Plot, and what was believed to have been Queen Henrietta Maria's popish plot in the 1630s, at which Charles I and Archbishop Laud were held to have connived. It was widely believed that Catholics could obtain papal authorisation for taking oaths of loyalty which they had no intention of keeping. All this did not prevent Protestant and Catholic gentlemen getting on amicably in their counties, nor did it prevent Milton from enjoying the hospitality of cardinals when he visited Rome. But the *institution* of the Roman Church could not be tolerated. Catholicism, Milton said, was not a religion but a political conspiracy. Bunyan and many others associated all persecution with the Antichrist.

The beleaguered Irish were seen as participants in the international popish plot against England. In the 1590s there were Spanish armies in Ireland supporting an Irish rebellion; in the 1640s Irish rebels were commanded by an Archbishop sent from Rome for that purpose. In the 1690s, again, James II, in alliance with Louis XIV, aimed to recover his throne in England via Ireland. Rivalry with France and Spain continued to be seen in religious terms well into the eighteenth century, when Frederick the Great was (to us rather implausibly) hailed as a Protestant hero. Catholic emancipation was facilitated by the French Revolution, after which Anglo-French colonial rivalry looked even less like a religious conflict. Earlier, Catholic emancipation in England would have seemed like the emancipation of Antichrist.

Neither Bunyan nor George Fox made grand statements on the principle of toleration. Both would have rejected the idea of their 'sect' being tolerated. They believed that theirs was the church of Christ, and demanded freedom to proclaim it. 'The laws of man can but settle a sect', declared the Quaker Edward Burrough; 'true religion can never be settled by that means'. Intolerance, he argued, led necessarily to hypocrisy. Hence, like Milton, he insisted on the widest freedom for all Protestants. Enforced uniformity was antichristian.

The word 'toleration' means acceptance of something on a temporary basis, something not in itself desirable. The Edict of Nantes granted toleration to Huguenots in France, but it was always a grudging toleration, and the Edict was revoked in 1685. English radicals wanted 'liberty of conscience' rather than 'toleration', freedom to believe *and* to organise as they wished. They rejected the idea of a compulsory national church in favour of voluntary congregations which might (or might not) be part of a loosely organised national church. Conservatives thought this would lead to confusion and anarchy. The parish was inextricably associated with local government, and in fact dissenters had – in defeat – to accept exclusion from local and central government after 1660 as well as exclusion from the universities which trained the clergy for the national church. In short, toleration came not because men became wider and nicer, but because circumstances had changed. Toleration comes only when men become indifferent to the issues involved. If those issues were serious, then the virtue of toleration is the result of the vice of indifference. But what the historian has to explain is *why* men and women became indifferent to what had once seemed – literally – life-and-death issues.

Indifference from below came when heretics were no longer ordered (under threat of violence) to believe what they could not believe. Belief is not totally voluntary: standards of faith change with social conditions. We may compare the ending of the use of torture in treason trials – not because it was now felt to be wrong, but because it was seen to be unnecessary as, for instance, better rules of evidence were elaborated. Burning heretics was discontinued because (amongst other reasons) it roused too much sympathy for the victims, and so no longer discouraged the others. Some martyrs in Mary's reign were themselves in principle in favour of burning heretics. The wide extension of printed material and the possibility of discussion among the articulate led to rethinking here. John Owen and Oliver Cromwell both advocated toleration when their own party was in power. So what were the changes in conditions? I have nothing very original to suggest here, but it may help to bring together familiar facts and to suggest inter-connections.

1. Expansion of world trade led to closer contacts with Islam and Jews in the Middle East, and with the ancient civilisations of India, China and Japan, as well as with Africa and America. It had to be recognised that Christianity was not unique: vast areas of the world existed in which its truths were unknown, but which nevertheless had attained a level of civilisation at least comparable with that of Europe. Men also learnt that Turks were more tolerant than Christians. Sir Henry Blount's *Voyage into the Levant* (1636) compared Islam favourably with Christianity. When Turks invaded Germany in 1663, the Rev. Ralph Josselin was only mildly shocked by some saying that they hoped the Turks would overrun Christianity, because then they would gain their liberty. That was going a bit far, Josselin thought. Nevertheless he believed that 'God may do good' by the Turks. Conservatives used the tolerance of the Turks as an argument *against* allowing toleration in a Christian country.

2. Toleration was a practical necessity if money was to be made through international trade – as the Turks had learnt, and as freebooters operating in the West Indies soon learnt too. The Navigation Act of 1651, confirmed after the restoration, set England's sights on controlling the trade of the world: the economic argument for toleration was powerful in seventeenth-century

England. Archbishop Laud's intolerance of Dutch and Walloon refugees had ruined the clothing industry of Kent. It was reversed when Parliament met. The Act of Uniformity of 1662 was observed to benefit our trade rival the Netherlands by driving skilled artisans into emigration, and by then articulate MPs were there to draw attention to the harm done. The fact that dissenters came mostly from the trading sector of the population strengthened the argument for toleration.

3. Recognition of the existence of other civilisations and other religions led, in the freedom of the forties and fifties, to thoughts about comparative religion. The Koran was published in English translation in 1649. It worried Bunyan greatly. All sorts of new mental horizons were opened up. In the mid-fifties Jews were readmitted to England after 350 years of absence. Economic arguments were mainly responsible. The uniqueness of the Bible, and its authority and reliability, were all open for discussion. By the second half of the century this was a subject of jokes in restoration comedy. When Lady Brute in Vanbrugh's *The Provoked Wife* was faced with the Biblical injunction to love our enemies, her answer came pat: 'that may be a mistake in the translation'. By the end of the century Mary Astell could respond to the old argument in favour of the inferiority of women – that God created Adam before he created Eve – by the simple observation that God created the animals before Adam. What should we conclude from that? Personal experience in colonial Surinam led the novelist Aphra Behn to create the noble savage, and to allow him to laugh at the Trinity.

4. The new astronomy also cast doubts on the uniqueness of this earth, and consequently on the uniqueness of Christianity. The new science came into its own after 1640, when the writings of Bacon and others were popularised. Charles Webster has emphasised the encouragement of science by interregnum governments, an encouragement which Charles II was wise enough to continue.

5. Thus, the ferment of discussion in the revolutionary decades compounded the effects of the expansion of knowledge of the world and the universe. A single state church of which all Englishmen and women were members simply broke down, and so did its censorship. Twenty years of consumers' choice in religion, based on free discussion, could not be obliterated. Theorists of toleration

like Lord Brooke, Walwyn and Milton were reacting to these circumstances. Theirs was a society in which mobility was suddenly accelerated by the civil war, armies carried the culture of the metropolis to the 'dark corners of the land', and found sometimes unexpected allies waiting for them. It was impossible ever to return to the intellectual world of pre-1640. The country yokel John Bunyan unlearned and learned everything during his two and a half years of garrison service in the town of Newport Pagnell, where the radical discussions of the rank and file caused the gravest alarm to its commanding officer.

6. The years 1640–60 made dissent too strong to be crushed or harried out of the land, as had been seriously intended before 1640. On the other hand dissenters realised that they were not strong enough to control the state without perpetual war and suffering, without ruin and disruption of the families of the small-shopkeeper class. They were themselves, they found by bitter experience, hopelessly divided. Here was the dissidence of dissent. Moderate dissenters long continued to hope for comprehension within the national church. All dissenters came ultimately to accept partial freedom, religious rather than political. The English nation ceased to be co-terminous with the Church of England. After 1689 it was discovered that the existence of two nations did not mean anarchy, or loss of government control. Once dissenters had accepted their position as a subordinate part of the nation, with freedom of religious worship at the expense of exclusion from central and local government and from the universities, a *modus vivendi* could be worked out. Exclusion from local and national government meant that dissenters lost the support of the gentry which had been such a feature of earlier puritanism. A gentleman had to be able to represent his county on the bench and in Parliament. The two nations were socially divided. Recognition that Christ's kingdom was not of this world, the failure of revolutionary millenarianism, of the rule of the saints, was a great turning point, the consequence of the trial and failure of the radical revolution. The dissenting interest became the trading interest.

The Church of England after 1640 never recovered the position of economic and political dominance to which the Laudians had aspired. Bishops came back in 1660, but they had no High Commission Court to enforce unpopular policies by branding and ear-slicing. Excommunication ceased to be an effective sentence because it was unenforceable against the vast dissenting population. 'It was only their not going to church', one employer reassured his employees. Who would mind that, now that fines for non-attendance were ineffective, and jobs were easily available elsewhere in the increasingly mobile society?

The solidarity of dissent had long been demonstrated. Dissenters had learnt to take full economic advantage of family and church connections in their business transactions. Before 1640 Nehemiah Wallington was able to find support and protection among the godly of East Anglia when forced to leave London. Town corporations had shown their ability to put group solidarity about political considerations in their resistance to the major-generals' rule in 1655–6. They showed the same solidarity in response to the purges initiated after 1660, and again in the 1680s. Charles II, who wanted to tolerate dissenters and so win their support for the crown, was a better analyst of the situation than the bishops and many MPs who wanted to take a hard line against dissenters. Dissenters, or most of them, now asked only to be left alone: erratic and spasmodic persecution was for them the worst of all possible fates. The wisdom of the king's policy was recognised by the Toleration Act of 1689.

7. Abandonment of the millenarian hope, of the rule of the saints, combined with the declining belief in hell analysed by D. P. Walker, achieved what Hobbes had thought essential for civil peace: an end to effective belief in rewards and punishments in the afterlife – the greatest stimulus, in his view, to determined revolutionary activity.[9] Soon after the restoration Henry More spoke of talk of Antichrist not as dangerous but as vulgar, unfit for polite conversation. When John Mason announced that the end of the world was to begin in Water Stratford in 1694, and drew large crowds there, he was not prosecuted: he was advised to take physic.

8. By the end of the seventeenth century it had come to be appreciated that market forces were more effective in controlling dissent than erratic state terror. As with the press, totally effective censorship was beyond the capacities of the government. A printing press was a cheap and portable piece of equipment. It was impossible to prevent the smuggling into the country from abroad of illegal literature. The would-be police state was woefully

inefficient by modern standards. The Licensing Act was allowed to lapse in 1695 because publishers could now be relied on in their own interests not to publish seditious material. Ludlow's and Milton's prose was reprinted from the revolutionary era, not the writings of Levellers, Diggers and Ranters. When Quakers reprinted the works of their founding fathers, they omitted most of the pamphlets from which I have quoted. Quakers themselves restrained their rank and file from indulging in the wilder gestures – disrupting services, going naked for a sign – that had seemed necessary in the face of the imminent millennium. The Toleration Act, by repeating Charles II's arrangements for licensing non-conformist congregations, gave some government control. It was exercised through the congregations themselves, and so was more efficient. Toleration proved a more effective way of controlling dissent than persecution. Locke supplied a satisfactory theory, drawing on way-out radical writings of half a century earlier, but the main impetus may have come from practical expedience rather than from philosophy.

So my suggestion is not just that toleration results from indifference, but rather that the breakdown of one type of authoritarianism tends to lead to the temporary victory of another authoritarianism. Only when both sides have exhausted themselves can the possibility of *neither* winning outright be grasped, and the small voice of reason make itself heard.

Notes

1. 'A Few Sighs From Hell, or The Groans of a Damned Soul', *The Works of John Bunyan*, ed. George Offor, Blackie and Son, 1858, Vol. III, pp. 666–724.
2. 'The Heavenly Footman', *The Works of John Bunyan*, Vol. III, p. 394.
3. 'A Few Sighs From Hell', pp. 695–6.
4. Edward Fowler, later Bishop of Gloucester. See Christopher Hill, *A Tinker and a Poor Man: John Bunyan and His Church, 1628–1688,* New York, Knopf, 1989, p. 105.
5. See Christopher Hill, 'Quakers and the English Revolution', in Michael Mullett (ed.), *New Light on George Fox, 1624–1691: A Collection of Essays,* York, William Sessions, 1993, pp. 22–35.
6. Samuel Fisher, *The Testimony of Truth Exalted*, 1679. See also Hill, *A Tinker and a Poor Man*, p. 85, and Christopher Hill, *The World Turned Upside Down,* Harmondsworth, Penguin, 1984, p. 259ff.

7. For more on the bellicose language used by early Quakers see Hill, 'Quakers and the English Revolution'.
8. For more on the rise of Quaker pacifism see Hill, *The World Turned Upside Down*, Chapter 10, 'Ranters and Quakers'.
9. D. P. Walker, *The Decline of Hell: Seventeenth Century Discussions of Eternal Torment*, London, Routledge and Kegan Paul, 1964.

Chapter 4

Tolerating religion
George Carey

How can religion itself be tolerated? No serious commentator on world events today can discount the significance of religion – whether in Eastern Europe, Southern Africa, Latin America or the Middle East. So we have to learn how to come to terms with, how to tolerate, religion. And we must also learn how religion itself may be tolerating, that is to say, accommodating of that over against which it stands. Religion will not disappear. It may well be that those who say we should expect a resurgence of religion in the West are right. But conjectures aside, what is undeniably the case is that many societies are now becoming increasingly pluralistic. Different faiths exist side by side in many more places in the world than a century ago. Britain, which once knew only Judaism as a minority faith, is no longer as predominantly Christian as it was: Islam, Hinduism, Jainism and other Eastern faiths are present in growing numbers. It is perplexing to many, so it is timely to ask: What is the nature of a tolerating religion? Can it get on with others and on what basis? And there are questions, too, for the secular citizen, who has no faith at all or, at best, is only a nominal Christian adherent. To this person the question is addressed: what place do any faith communities have in our secular world? On what basis do we tolerate them?

First, however, the concept of tolerance itself needs to be defined. The dictionaries do not take us very far: 'to put up with' or 'to permit' both suggest a deprecating attitude towards something which is not wholly approved. Perhaps we cannot both 'like' and 'tolerate' something at the same time. The terms are mutually exclusive. A domestic analogy might fill in the picture at one level. I have a teenage daughter who loves pop music. You know she is at home when the house erupts with noise. The nearer you get to her room, the greater the danger to your ear drums and the lower your tolerance level of the music. But that doesn't mean I don't love my daughter. Such an issue does not defeat the lasting quality of the relationship simply because what is bonding us is so much greater than this minor irritation.

However, domestic illustrations do not help us to see how it is that passions can be held so deeply that people will suffer for them, and persecute, rather than tolerate, in the name of them. Here, another modern analogy might help. We talk often of tolerance of pain. We may pride ourselves on being able to have our teeth filled without an injection if our pain threshold is high. Or, to quote Bacon's splendid *Apothegm* on Tolerance, with its double meaning: 'Diogenes, one terrible frosty morning, came into the Market-Place, and stood Naked, shaking, to show his Tolerance.'[1] Perhaps this helps us towards a better definition. 'Tolerance' has something to do with intensity of commitment: it is the 'obverse' of commitment's 'reverse'. There are those whose commitment to their goals, God or values are such that no cost is too great for them to bear in order to achieve them. Pain and sacrifice are gladly borne by them.

This link between tolerance and pain is important. Tolerant people do not attempt to impose their opinions by external pressure or enforce them by any means except thoughtful persuasion. But this only holds true where people actually *have* opinions. People with no convictions are not being tolerant if they allow others their way or if they acquiesce with the opinions of others. They are simply 'in-different'. The very word 'apathetic' expresses this. It refers to someone who does not 'feel the pain', and for our society this needs to be emphasised. *Indifference is not toleration.* People steeped in the laziness of mental or moral indifference sometimes pride themselves on their tolerance. They are not tolerant. Indifference is never a virtue. The indifferent exercise no self-restraint. They don't have to cultivate humility when faced with a clash of values. They don't have to balance the demands of their integrity against respect for the

convictions of others. There is no moral struggle. Ogden Nash put it
so well:

> Sometimes with secret pride I sigh
> to think how tolerant am I;
> Then wonder which is really mine:
> Tolerance or a rubber spine?

Baroness Wooton observed similarly: 'People are tolerant only about
things they don't really care about'. But true tolerance implies
convictions and deeply held values.

The history of tolerance has sometimes been dismissed as a
terrible story of religious people tearing one another apart in the
service and love of God. I am often asked how I justify that, and the
simple answer is of course that I do not, and have no wish to try. I
would never want to justify those who believe it right to persecute
and kill others whose convictions are just as honorably held. But
before we take the high moral ground let us remember that in this
century alone more people have been persecuted and killed for their
beliefs and differences than perhaps in all other centuries put
together. And most of these deaths have not come from religious
conflicts. Atheistic ideologies have proved astonishingly capable of
sending millions to their deaths. We moderns have very little to
boast about.

In the history of religious toleration, I believe there are three
phases. These I describe as the emergence of individualism, the
attempt at establishment, and the development of co-existence.

The emergence of individualism

Lambeth Palace, my London home and office, echoes with
reminders of intolerance. I am surrounded by portraits which
recall how many brave people have been willing to lay down
their lives for what they believed to be God's truth. Archbishop
Cranmer, who died at the stake in the time of Queen Mary;
archbishop, William Laud, whose cause was too tightly tied to
Charles I, and was taken from his prayers to the Tower of London

and his eventual execution. Then there is Cardinal Pole, the last Roman Catholic Archbishop who died but a few days after Mary Tudor, perhaps just missing a martyr's crown. Then in the Lollards Tower at Lambeth Palace there is one of the saddest rooms in London: eight iron chains testify to people once held in the Lollards prison because they followed the teachings of John Wycliffe. Their fourteenth-century names are carved into the woodwork. Yet the martyrs and the persecutors (and Lambeth's art and architecture reminds us how often the sides change) would not have used the word 'intolerance'. All were convinced that God's truth could be found, that they had found it, and that it was vitally important for the life of the nation that it should be held, embraced and believed, just as *they* held, embraced and believed it. There were no half measures, no time for qualifications. Passion led them forward and they were willing to bear the pain. Such was the indivisibility of state and religion that the persecution of the heretic was considered a necessary and inevitable consequence of such religious individualism. If individuals could believe what they liked, and proclaim what they believed, society would collapse. Religious freedom and anarchy were identified. Heresy had to be eliminated from the state just as much as from the church. The soul of the heretic could only be saved by persuasion, by torture to correct beliefs, and perhaps by death. The medieval mind some-times even understood the burning of heretics to be the loving thing to do. Purified by a few moments of earthly fire, the heretic might thus avoid a greater conflagration. It does not seem a convincing argument to the modern mind.

Although it is sometimes said and believed that it was a gradual religious indifference which led to genuine toleration, the seeds were already present in the very conflict, for the Reformation was a witness to the emergence of the *individual*. Personal response to the love of God was decisive. Justification depended on faith, not the faith of the church as a whole, but the faith of each of its members. As John McManners notes: 'Religion was on its way to becoming a matter of intense personal decision; if there was a single message and driving force behind Reformation and Counter-Reformation, it was this. Secularization was the inevitable counterpart, the opposite side of the coin, the reaction of human nature to a demand almost too intense to bear.'[2] If then faith is a matter of intense personal decision it cannot be forced from reluctant people. It has to be owned, accepted and believed.

The attempt at establishment

The aftermath of the Reformation with its unhappy history of religious wars led not to religious liberty but to an uneasy peace. The attempt at establishment meant the creation of separate religious states each with its distinctive religious ethos as the bond of the tribe. The principle was *'cujus regio ejus religio'*, to each region its own religion. This of course was tolerance for governments rather than for the individual, who still had to conform to the dominant faith where she or he lived. The most liberal thing you can do in such circumstances is to make your single church as wide and as comprehensive as possible, but even in England where the established church did make such an attempt – and still claims to be comprehensive – unreconciled parties were left in the wings, unable in all conscience to accept the *modus vivendi*. Such a situation could not last very long because individual conscience could no longer be suppressed once the Reformation had liberated it. Seventeenth-century England shows the policy collapsing through the pressure brought to bear by two religious systems, Episcopalian and Presbyterian, each claiming to be the right faith for English society. They were fighting to decide the character of the English nation in its capacity as an organised religious society. Contrary to the way Oliver Cromwell has been depicted, it was he who established a tolerance that was in fact wider than he dared openly to avow. He adopted a tolerant attitude to Jews who were already living in the country and gave private assurances to them that the recusancy laws would not be put into operation against them, even though he judged the time was not ripe to remove such laws. This *genuine* toleration (as distinct from eighteenth-century indifferentism to which I shall refer later) was endorsed powerfully at the end of the century by Locke. In his 1689 *Letter on Toleration* he wrote, 'Since you are pleased to enquire what are my thoughts about the mutual Toleration of Christians in their different Professions of Religion, I must needs answer you freely, that I esteem that toleration to be the chief Characteristical Mark of the True Church'.

The development of co-existence

Thus we see heralded the development of co-existence. The territorial idea of religion simply gave way under the force of those whose commitment and pain prevented them accepting an enforced religion. Precisely because religion was so supremely important, it came to be held that one man could not impose it upon another and even a whole society could not impose it upon an individual. So William Penn, one of the great founding fathers in the New World, wrote in 1685:

> All forms of persons are for liberty of conscience for themselves, even those that are most imposing upon others. As a variety of flowers may grow on the same bank, so may Protestants and Papists live in England. Union in affection is not inconsistent with disagreement of opinion. We cannot come together in the same church but may live in the same land and as we are under the same gracious King, he may protect both and suffer no party to persecute one another.[3]

It was weariness with controversy about tolerance, and acts of real intolerance, that led persecuted groups to seek asylum in the new world to create their own societies in which people might be free to worship and live as they please. Thus from passionate commitment to worship God freely, there arose, in possibly the most religious society in the world, the separation of state and religion.

However, we must not fall into the trap of thinking that toleration was achieved with the emigration of the Pilgrim Fathers. The eighteenth and nineteenth centuries were times of *co-existence*, not genuine tolerance. Even up to very recent times in Western Christianity we have examples of attitudes where little was changed. It is worth tracing the more recent history of this in the Roman Catholic Church, for instance, to see how lately 'toleration' has been understood as a necessity of, not a threat to, faith.

We may begin with Monsignor Ronald Knox, the famous Roman Catholic intellectual, who in his *The Belief of Catholics* trenchantly argued that the very truth of the Catholic faith meant that, in a country with a strong Catholic majority, the church must insist on Catholic education being universal and would proscribe those who come with deviant teachings. He stated: 'A body of Catholic patriots entrusted with the government of a Catholic State, will not shrink even from repressive measures in order to perpetuate the secure domination of Catholic principles among their fellow-countrymen.' Against the view that this is intolerant, Knox continued in swashbuckling fashion: 'When we demand liberty in the modern state we are appealing to its own principles not to ours. The theory of the modern state is that all religions should be tolerated, as long as they do not disturb the peace or otherwise infringe the secular laws of the country; we only claim to share that right amongst the rest.'[4] We must allow for the fact that Knox was well known for his over-statements, but even so the claim reveals that 'genuine toleration' was far from his mind.

Moreover, the double standard inherent in Knox's response was a classic Roman Catholic argument prior to the Second Vatican Council, stemming from the views of Bishop Felix Dupanloup of Orleans and distinguishing between 'thesis' and 'hypothesis'. The 'thesis' was that when Catholicism was in power, error should be repressed. Only when Catholicism was not dominant should error be tolerated as a lesser evil. That was the 'hypothesis', and before we condemn and criticise this argument as peculiarly Roman Catholic, we have to recognise that such a view has *never* been exclusively Catholic or even exclusively religious. Many ideological movements as well as religious groups have claimed a freedom when in a minority which they have not been prepared to concede to others when in power. (Milton, when faced with the behaviour of the very Presbyterians he had helped to put in power in England, wrote bitterly, 'New presbyter is but old priest writ large.')

However, this view was already changing before the Second Vatican Council pronounced firmly against it which, let no one doubt, it *firmly* did. It was the great Jesuit thinker John Courtney

Murray who argued that religious freedom, far from being a necessary evil (as the 'thesis/hypothesis' argument put it), is a personal and
political *good*. Murray distinguished between 'freedom of conscience'
and 'free exercise of religion'. Freedom of conscience meant im-
munity against external coercion; free exercise of religion meant that
in a free society all faiths must have equality of expression and the
protection of the law.[5] Behind this lay the profound truth that a
forced faith is no faith at all. The Second Vatican Council's landmark
document *Dignitatis Humanae* (Declaration of Religious Freedom)
codified Murray's philosophical ideals and explicitly acknowledged
the fact of the religiously plural society.

This necessarily brief survey suggests that, at best, genuine tolerance is only a recent reality. My contention is that it is still not
securely founded, and we have a long way to go before it can be
considered a genuine fact in modern society and in personal life. To
get to the heart of the matter, therefore, we must consider the
dynamics of tolerance.

The dynamics of tolerance

It is simplistic to think that tolerance is achieved merely by a
shoulder-shrugging indifference to people who believe and act
differently. That attitude is not tolerance, it is apathy. Genuine
religious toleration is achieved when people hold their religion as so
important, so absolute, that to part from it is to die, and yet at the
same time realise from their absolute centre of being that *another*
person's values and beliefs are just as important and just as real. That
is the moment of genuine tolerance, because there is a cost involved
in the act of tolerating another person's way of living and believing.
The pain involved is not only in preserving inviolate one's own
convictions, but in enduring the reality of other people's and, whilst
deeply disagreeing, respecting them – with a consequent sharing of
their pain as well as one's own. In my enthronement sermon the
word I used was 'integrity' – the act of recognising that a strong and
robust faith does not necessarily flow into intolerance and hostility
but can mean respecting another whose commitment is just as deep
but is different.

Let me quote Elizabeth Templeton, that fine Presbyterian theologian, on the issue that currently seems to engender *in*tolerance in the Church of England – the ordination of women. 'I have been constantly struck', she said at the Lambeth Conference of 1988:

> by the best generosity of your Anglican recurrent insistence that across parties, camps, styles and dogmas, you have need of one another . . . I am sad you feel you are under some pressure to renounce this remarkable openness of being . . . My hope is that you can see the issue of women's ordination as a gift . . . not just because it opens up deep and wide theological questions, but because it also touches the levels of pain and passion which test what it means that we love our enemies. The world is used to unity of all sorts, to solidarity in campaigns . . . communities of party, creed, interest. But it is *not* used to such possibilities as this: that, for example, those who find the exclusion of women from the priesthood an intolerable apartheid, and those who find their inclusion a violation of God's will, *should enter one another's suffering*. Somewhere in there authority lies.

'Somewhere in there authority lies.' In there, where we tolerate pain – each other's and our own. That is the dynamic and new understanding of toleration I seek to share with you, because it is what as a society as well as a church we need to learn. It is in that dynamic and suffering tolerance that we gain in 'authority' as a nation, for tolerance involves entering into the 'strangeness' of others and feeling their pain.

Tolerance and strangeness

Let us put this on a less lofty level, applying it to daily life. Minorities always feel persecuted, alone, outnumbered and misunderstood. Majorities usually regard minorities as prickly and over-sensitive, introverted and always on about their rights. Both views are accurate to a degree and both are due to the element of 'strangeness' we experience when, for instance, we are tourists and visiting a foreign country. After all, one of the reasons we travel is to experience such strangeness. However, 'strangeness' can lead to 'alienation', something very dangerous, especially if the stranger becomes our neighbour, bringing different smells, clothes, speech and behaviour into close proximity. And that alienation may be deepened when the stranger takes over shops and jobs and becomes a competitor. The scene is then set for conflict. The strange minority may become the focus of pent-up frustrations and bitternesses which have little to do with them.

Differences can only be overcome when they are recognised as potential enrichments to our society and lives, even when there is a high price to pay. It may start with a genuine liking for Indian cooking. That may lead to an enquiry about why people dress as they do; about what goes on in a Hindu temple; about the lifestyle of these people whose strangeness is both fascinating and disturbing. People who live in a monochrome culture need to be made aware of the exciting possibilities, as well as the disturbances to their settled lifestyle, of a multicultural society. And that can only come about as we discover that 'strangeness' does not necessarily mean 'bad' but can be a different expression of 'good'.

Tolerance, understanding and education

Charles Raven records an episode during the war which started out well and nearly became a tragedy. In the autumn of 1940 a fenland village near Ely had arranged to put up a number of children from Bethnal Green. The families sent to them happened to come from a Jewish club. The economics and diet of the villagers centred, as it used to in the older rural areas, upon the household pig. In welcoming their honoured guests the treasured rashers were generously offered, in complete ignorance of Jewish food rules. To the older children and to the supervisor who escorted them, such an offering seemed a calculated insult. They were outraged. All sorts of authorities became involved. Both sides were deeply offended. What should have been a memorable yet happy day ended in near riot. The Jewish group, so oppressed by the terrible events happening to their people elsewhere in Europe, saw this as yet another element of persecution. The villagers were bruised that their great act of charity was flung in their face by what seemed to be a trivial matter of eating. It is an example of how ignorance and misunderstanding can produce situations which poison human relationships.

Ignorance exacerbates the problem of strangeness. We might reflect on the misunderstanding of the passionate reaction of the Muslim community to Salman Rushdie's *Satanic Verses*. Many non-Muslims who read the book could not understand what lay behind such passion because *our* tendency is to view a novel as a 'fictitious exploration of reality'. So 'fictional blasphemy' is not, and in the opinion of many secular people cannot be, 'blasphemy' at all. To that we have to add that to many people whose values are wholly secular there can be no such thing as 'blasphemy' since you cannot insult a God who does not exist. The devout Muslim, however, does not see it this way. The book contained an outrageous slur on the Prophet and so was damaging to the reputation of the faith. I well understand the devout Muslims' reaction, wounded by what they hold most dear and would themselves die for. Because we are strangers to Islam, and many of us to any concept of holiness at all, we do not feel the offence, the pain – and there we are, back with the image of pain, with *our* reaction, one of indifference. But Christians, like Muslims, living in an increasingly secular world, are likely themselves to encounter this pain more and more. For instance, the film *The Last Temptation of Christ* contains scenes that would shock and outrage many Christians, and the possibility that there could be real inability to understand or *tolerate* the distress caused to Christians by the film ought to help us better to enter the distress of the Muslim community.

Only sensitive understanding of the value structures of others will lead us into the tolerant society we seek for ourselves and our children. The same kindness and forbearance we want for our own integrity and lifestyle, we should offer to others. It is our ignorance and prejudice which so often get in the way, as well as our unwillingness to bear the pain of the cost.

Tolerance and freedom

Linked with tolerance is freedom. To tolerate another means to make him free to follow his conscience and exercise his freedom in whatever way suits him within the boundaries of the law. It follows that when we talk of the 'free world' we must make sure we know what we mean, to be warned of dangers to our freedom, and to note ways in which our freedom may be deepened. But freedom is a transcultural, universal idea. We want all people to enjoy it. We are glad that the forms of mental, moral and philosophical servitude which existed behind the Iron Curtain are no more, but freedom is surely much more than simply the individual's right to think and be. Freedom and toleration combined offer us several challenges.

First, the free person cannot tolerate injustices and evils in the world. For example, we ought not to be complacent about our nation's 'freedom' when so many people are homeless. Although efforts are being made to address the causes which create homelessness, for those reduced to such circumstances 'freedom' is curtailed. Or, to give another example, how can we talk easily about freedom when so many people in our world are starving and are the victims of war, natural disasters and economic systems not of their making? This involves countries like ours in the spreading of freedom, including *economic* freedom. Freedom is not defended by building walls around a state, but by being exported to those who lack it. It is exported when richer countries share the fruits of freedom with countries where there is great poverty and hunger. For Russia and the Eastern Bloc political freedom will only be secure if their economies improve and grow secure. The West has a duty to help them at this moment, lest their desperation produces another tyranny should they sense we abandon them.

Second, in the religious domain, freedom is the fruit of toleration. John Courtney Murray isolated three aspects of human dignity and freedom, and he distinguished between the 'common good' and 'public order'. The 'common good' includes all the social, spiritual and moral goods which people need to live and which together we must strive to achieve. Public order, on the other hand, includes three goods which the state must supply: public peace, public morality and public justice. Murray comments that the first thing due to people in *justice* is their freedom, the proper enjoyment of their personal and social rights. 'Let there be as much freedom, personal and social, as possible; let there only be as much coercion and constraint, personal

and social, as may be necessary for the public order.' The truly
tolerant religious person therefore is led to embrace, not grudgingly
but gladly, the view that those who differ from him or her have every
right to worship as they choose. This in turn poses a challenge to
which we shall turn later: Does this not commit us to a recognition of
a universality of faiths?

The distinctive contribution of christianity

I turn now to consider the nature of Christianity's contribution to the
search for a genuinely tolerant society. We have seen that although it
was itself a persecuted minority for the first three hundred years or so,
the freedom it sought for itself it has not always desired to give to
others. Christianity's own search for tolerance has dark shadows, and
some fundamentalist groups repel thoughtful people by their language of intolerance.

The distinctive contribution of Christianity to the discovery of a
dynamic tolerance of the kind I envisaged as a hope for our age arises
from the very nature of God himself as Christians understand Him.
The words 'tolerating' and 'tolerant', when used of the nature of
God, are more frequently translated in modern versions of the Bible
as 'forbearing', 'longsuffering', 'patient', 'enduring'. It is that aspect of
God which, complementing the absoluteness of His power, exercises
gentleness and longsuffering even with those who abuse Him or
confront Him. It is what the writer of Peter describes as 'forbearing,
not wishing that any should perish'; or the writer of Numbers or
Exodus described as 'longsuffering': the 'Lord God merciful and
gracious, longsuffering and abounding in steadfast love'. Incarnate,
we find an expression of it in Christ's reported words in Mark 9.19
when the crowd were being more than usually unperceiving; 'un-
believing generation', he says, 'How long shall I stay with you? How
long shall I put up with you?' As one very perceptive commentator
remarked, His being with men involved Him in 'putting up with
them'. It involved tolerating them. It is the complement of the
heavenly majesty that Christians claim as rightly Christ's. And
Christians would argue that humankind, recalled to its proper self
through the action of God's love, must also display this quality that

complements the royalty of the redeemed nature which is God's gift. That tolerance which 'truly bears and takes to oneself one's neighbour' lies in the sense of fully or wholly and feelingly tolerating the life of the other person. As Walt Whitman has written:

> We hear the bawling and the din, we are reached by divisions, jealousies, recriminations on every side,
> They close peremptorily upon us to surround us, my Comrade,
> Yet we walk upheld, free, the whole world over, journeying up and down till we make our ineffaceable mark upon the time and the diverse eras . . .
> That the men and women of races, ages to come,
> may prove at last brethren lovers.

This glimpse of the Christian understanding of the nature of God and its implications for the distinctive contribution that mainstream churches could make today to the life of our world, leads me to identify three main qualities we ought to look for, which should inform the dynamic toleration of which I speak.

The first lies in the value of magnanimity. Paul in Philippians 4.5 writes: 'Let your magnanimity [*epieikeia*] be known to all people.' The word expresses breadth, the quality of taking in as much as possible. Aristotle describes the meaning of '*epieikeia*': 'it is *epieikeia* to pardon human feelings and look to the lawgiver not to the law, to the spirit not to the letter, to the intention not to the action, to the whole and not to the part . . . To remember good rather than evil.' Christians should be able to find the pattern of magnanimity in the Lord they follow because in this pattern of teaching and living the way of tolerance is observable in His delight in people, in His protection of the defenceless, and in His refusal to take up arms against those who differed from Him. Christ rebukes sternly the two intolerant disciples who wanted fire from heaven to destroy a Samaritan village which refused their message. That was not His way. His was the way of the cross. The truly magnanimous person is he who gives to another space to grow; who is so secure in his own faith that he is not threatened by another's spirituality or difference of view. It is often small-minded, fear-ridden people who cannot tolerate others.

The second quality which informs the dynamic of toleration is the nature of love or 'charity'. Mainstream Christianity emphasises the personal because of the Christocentric nature of its mission. Central to Christianity is the conviction that God has taken human existence into His life because the divine took human form and suffered for us. William Temple's quip that 'Christianity is the most materialistic of all religions' has its roots in that theology. God's love for all people finds its origin here, and it may possibly be the case that Paul's glorious paean of praise to 'charity' in 1. Corinthians.13 is derived from a meditation on the person of Christ Himself: 'Charity suffers long and is kind; charity envies not; charity vaunts not itself, does not behave itself unseemly, is not easily provoked, thinks no evil, rejoices not in iniquity but rejoices in the truth; charity bears all things, believes all things, hopes all things, endures all things.' Paul's beautiful words express a deep conviction about the worth of all people – that we are valued by God because we are loved by Him. The principle of charity will stop any group which has a high doctrine of exclusivity from becoming narrow-minded and intolerant.

The third quality informing the dynamic of toleration is the nature of *community* as '*koinonia*'. For genuine Christianity, belonging to the body of Christ takes the form of personal choice as well as God's call. The individual is not coerced but joins gladly. Yet by belonging we take upon ourselves obligations to share the Christian faith with others and to live out its moral obligations in society. I concede readily that there have been repressive Christian communities in the past and there are possibly some around even today. But the notion of a tolerant body of people who join together in mutual bonds of affection and service can be and is an inspiring model of community today. Such a body will recognise the rights of others and will be eager to learn, share in dialogue and debate and be willing to embrace new insights and new learning. And such a body will be open to the society in which it is earthed and so resistant to narrow-mindedness.

However, such a vision of Christianity faces two major challenges from a multicultural situation. The first is in relation to that 'exclusivity' which seems to deny the value of other faith communities. Recently, the press has carried stories of an 'Open Letter' to the leadership of the Church of England. It has not yet been published but its contents are well known. It comes from a group who fear that the Christian message is being vitiated by interfaith worship. They fear an *inclusivity* which rejects the uniqueness of Christ. They are worried that evangelism might be abandoned. Can one believe with integrity that Jesus Christ is the Way, the Truth and the Life and *still* believe that other faiths are not simply of value, but that they matter to God, or are in some way vehicles of salvation? There are many different levels at which we have to respond to that question and they cannot all be explored here. What we have to recognise is that because God is the kind of God He is, our integrity as believers in Him *compels* us to behave in such a way that tolerance, and not intolerance is our instinctive reaction, and that honest engagement with each other as valued by God becomes the context in which our differences are faced – and faced strenuously.

But it would be exceedingly disingenuous of all parties to throw up hands in horror at the thought of preaching an exclusive creed. Islam and Christianity have from the very beginning been quite open and explicit abut the nature of their faith. Both claim to be universal faiths and both are missionary. What has changed is that these faiths are no longer separated by thousands of miles, but we are now in one another's backyards, and we rightly feel the pain which is the other side of tolerance. Both religions, and other faiths too, must to be true to that justice which is of the nature of the God both faiths celebrate, and concede to each other the toleration our nation needs.

A second challenge relates to missionary tactics. A fresh humility is required by which the integrity of other faiths is recognised and their genuine contribution to the well-being of humankind honoured. One can, I believe, be a Christian wholly convinced of the uniqueness of Christ and his abiding relevance to humankind, and still affirm that other faiths possess value, significance and integrity. The Bossey Consultation of 1956 stated that 'all mission has the nature of dialogue'. Dialogue can only take place between those who value each other. Christians engaged in dialogue may thus approach their own faith in a new way. It opens up new and exciting opportunities to engage with the living faith of another and to have one's own faith enlarged and deepened by it. And that happens properly at the same time as we are sharing how our life is charged and sustained by our own faith in the God and Father of our Lord Jesus Christ.

Nonetheless, a pressing issue remains for a missionary faith such as Christianity. Evangelism is still a binding obligation on the Christian believer, so how does that relate to a pluralism of many faiths in which mutual respect and tolerance are prized? How does one avoid the pitfall of proselytising on the one hand and the negation of the task on the other? The answer must lie in acknowledging that although the task remains the same, the method of sharing faith will be different in our new context. As neighbours now, the cultural implications require the greatest sensitivity to those who are our fellow citizens: that dynamic tolerance which enters into the 'faith sufferings' of those whose faith is not ours, and yet retains integrity, true to its own convictions.

The implications of what I have said are of consequence for us all. I have painted a picture of an emerging world order in which religions are not a declining factor, but are growing side by side. We have to recognise the fear that our 'strangeness' can cause each other. 'Fanaticism' may be, as Shabbir Akhtar puts it, '*other people's* passions' (and by implication our own passion is 'faith'), but if adherence to religious principle threatens whole communities by the intensity of commitment, civilised society cannot and must not tolerate such an invasion of public order. And the reason for this is not because of liberal humanism, but because the profoundest toleration is rooted in the nature of God. Shabbir Akhtar's excellent book *A Faith for All Seasons* shows that different though Judaism, Christianity and Islam may be, they do possess common values and beliefs.[6] That should be the starting point of our common task to share our humanity together.

There are implications here for our secular world, which, bewildered by the profusion of religious belief, is tempted to throw up its hands in horror, cry 'A plague on both your houses', and get on with its task of living, without benefit of any religious faith at all. But the pluraformity of life which the secular state has to recognise forces it not only to observe the fact of minorities and to cater for them in its laws and in its life, but to respect and value them. All religions are not the same, as lawmakers and the media have found out to their cost, and their value-systems should not, and, thankfully cannot, be easily dismissed.

Ultimately, however, the chief implication challenges all religious leaders who are called not simply to an affable co-existence – a denial of true toleration – but an active partnership and deeper co-operation, which means entering into and sharing each other's 'pains'. Jonathan Sacks in *The Persistence of Faith* says strikingly: 'That is counter-fundamentalism, the belief that God has given us many universes of faith but only one world in which to live together.'[7] And in this overcrowded and rapidly exhausting little planet the need for cooperation and sharing is an urgent and necessary task. Resurgent faiths can no longer afford to exhaust their total strength simply on enlarging their frontiers but must be challenged to expend the same energy on the social face of faith – the enormous and growing numbers of the poor and starving and the ecological desert we are creating through misuse and exploitation. The Heavenly Father Christ describes is not one who, if asked for bread, would merely give a stone – even a Tablet of Stone.

My dominant image in this paper has been that of pain; pain of believers who learn in real situations that 'to tolerate' is not just the 'right thing to do' but the moral and just way to be. The genuinely tolerant are not those indifferent to others who believe different things. They are the ones who, themselves of passionate beliefs, endure the pain of that and enter into the pain others feel in their conflicting passionate beliefs. Only out of such mutuality of toleration will the dynamic come that gives freedom and space to all. It is my passionate conviction that when we are prepared to die for another's right to belief, in just the way we might be prepared to die for the right to our own, we might then have begun to explore the toleration of God. For it is His tolerating us which will make us all ultimately free as citizens of this country and of the one to come.

Notes

1. *The Essays of Lord Bacon including his Moral and Historical Works*, London, Frederick Warne and sons, p. 372.
2. John McManners, 'Enlightenment: Secular and Christian' in John McManners (ed.), *The Oxford Illustrated History of Christianity,* Oxford, Oxford University Press, 1990, p. 267.

3. William Penn, *Collected Works*, Joseph Besse, 1726, vol. II.
4. Ronald Knox, *The Belief of Catholics*, London, Sheed and Ward, 1939.
5. John Courtenay Murray, *We Hold These Truths: Catholic Reflections on the American Proposition*, London, Sheed and Ward, 1960.
6. Shabbir Akhtar, *A Faith for All Seasons*, London, Bellew, 1990.
7. Jonathan Sacks, *The Persistence of Faith*, London, Weidenfeld and Nicolson, 1991.

Chapter 5

Tolerating the intolerable
Bernard Williams

The difficulty with toleration is that it seems to be at once necessary and impossible. It is necessary where different groups have conflicting beliefs – moral, political or religious – and realise that there is no alternative to their living together; no alternative, that is to say, except armed conflict, which will not resolve their disagreements and will impose continuous suffering. These are the circumstances in which toleration is necessary. Yet in those same circumstances it may well seem impossible.

If violence and the breakdown of social co-operation are threatened in these circumstances, it is because people find others' beliefs or ways of life deeply unacceptable. In matters of religion, for instance (which, historically, was the first area in which the idea of toleration was used), the need for toleration arises because one of the groups, at least, thinks that the other is blasphemously, disastrously, obscenely wrong. The members of one group may also think, very often, that the leaders or elders of the other group are keeping the young, or perhaps the women, from enlightenment and liberation. In this case, they see it as not merely in their own group's interest, but in the interest of some in the other group, that the true religion (as they believe it to be) should prevail. It is because the disagreement goes this deep that the parties to it think that they cannot accept the existence of each other. We need to tolerate other people and their ways of life only in situations that make it very difficult to do so. Toleration, we may say, is required only for the intolerable. That is its basic problem.

We may think of toleration as an attitude that a more powerful group, or a majority, may have (or may fail to have) towards a less powerful group or a minority. In a country where there are many Christians and few Muslims, there may be a question whether the Christians tolerate the Muslims; the Muslims do not get the choice, so to speak, whether to tolerate the Christians or not. If the proportions of Christians and Muslims are reversed, so will be the direction of toleration. This is how we usually think of toleration, and it is natural to do so, because discussions of toleration have often been discussions of what laws should exist – in particular, laws permitting or forbidding various kinds of religious practice – and the laws have been determined by the attitudes of the more powerful group. But more basically, toleration is a matter of the attitudes of any group to another, and does not concern only the relations of the more powerful to the less powerful. It is certainly not just a question of what laws there should be. A group or a creed can rightly be said to be 'intolerant' if it would like to suppress or drive out others even if, as a matter of fact, it has no power to do so. The problems of toleration are to be first found at the level of human relations and of the attitude of one way of life towards another. It is not only a question of how the power of the state is to be used, though of course it supports and feeds a problem about that – a problem of political philosophy. However, we should be careful about making the assumption that what underlies a *practice* of toleration must be a personal *virtue* of toleration. All toleration involves serious difficulties, but it is the virtue that most drastically threatens to involve conceptual impossibility.

If there is to be a question of toleration, it is necessary that there should be *something to be tolerated*; there has to be some belief or practice or way of life that one group may think (however fanatically or unreasonably) to be wrong, or mistaken, or undesirable. If one group simply hates another, as with a clan vendetta or cases of sheer racism, it is not really toleration that is needed: the people involved need rather to lose their hatred, their prejudice, or their implacable memories. If we are asking people to be tolerant, we are asking for something more complicated than this. They will indeed have to lose something, their desire to suppress or drive out the rival belief; but they will also keep something, their commitment to their own beliefs, which is what gave them that desire in the first place. There is a tension here between one's own commitments and the acceptance that other people may have other and perhaps quite distasteful commitments. This is the tension that is typical of toleration, and the tension which makes it so difficult.

Just because it involves this tension between commitment to one's own outlook and acceptance of the other's, toleration is supposed to be more than mere weariness or indifference. After the European wars of religion in the sixteenth and seventeenth centuries had raged for years, people began to think that it must be better for the different Christian churches to co-exist. Various attitudes went with this development. Some people became sceptical about the distinctive claims of any church, and began to think that there was no truth, or at least no truth discoverable by human beings, about the validity of one church's creed as opposed to another's. Other people began to think that the struggles had helped them to understand God's purposes better: that He did not mind how people worshipped, so long as they did so in good faith within certain broad Christian limits. And in more recent times, a similar ecumenical spirit has extended beyond the boundaries of Christianity.

These two lines of thought in a certain sense went in opposite directions. One of them, the sceptical, claimed that there was less to be known about God's designs than the warring parties, each with its particular fanaticism, had supposed. The other line of thought, the broad church view, claimed to have a better insight into God's designs than the warring parties had. But in their relation to the battles of faith, the two lines of thought did nevertheless end up in the same position, with the idea that precise questions of Christian belief did not matter as much as people had supposed; that less was at stake. This leads to toleration as a matter of political *practice*, and that is an extremely important result. However, as an attitude, it is less than toleration. If you do not care all that much what anyone believes, you do not need the attitude of toleration, any more than you do with regard to other people's tastes in food.

In many matters, attitudes that are more tolerant in practice do arise for this reason, that people cease to think that a certain kind of behaviour is a matter for disapproval or negative judgement at all.

This is what is happening, in many parts of the world, with regard to kinds of sexual behaviour that were previously discouraged and in some cases legally punished. An extra-marital relationship or a homosexual ménage may arouse no hostile comment or reaction, as such things did in the past, but once again, though this is toleration as a matter of practice, the attitude it relies on is indifference rather than, strictly speaking, toleration. Indeed, if I and others in the neighbourhood said that we were *tolerating* the homosexual relations of the couple next door, our attitude would be thought to be less than liberal.

There are no doubt many conflicts and areas of intolerance for which the solution should indeed be found in this direction – in the increase of indifference. Matters of sexual and social behaviour which in smaller and more traditional societies are of great public concern will come to seem more a private matter, raising in themselves no question of right or wrong. The slide towards indifference may also provide, as it did in Europe, the only solution to some religious disputes. Not all religions, of course, have any desire to convert, let alone coerce, others. They no doubt have some opinion or other (perhaps of the 'broad church' type) about the state of truth or error of those who do not share their faith, but they are content to leave those other people alone. Other creeds, however, are less willing to allow error, as they see it, to flourish, and it may be that with them there is no solution except that which Europe discovered (in religion, at least, if not in politics) – a decline in enthusiasm. It is important that a decline of enthusiasm need not take the form of a movement's merely running out of steam. As the various sects of Christianity discovered, a religion may have its own resources for rethinking its relations to others. One relevant idea, which had considerable influence in Europe, is that an expansive religion really wants people to believe in it, but it must recognise that this is not a result that can be achieved by force. The most that force can achieve is acquiescence and outer conformity. As Hegel said of the slave's master, the fanatic is always disappointed: what he wanted was acknowledgement, but all he can get is conformity.

Scepticism, indifference or broad church views are not the only source of what I am calling toleration as a practice. It can also be secured in a Hobbesian equilibrium, under which the acceptance of one group by the other is the best that either of them can get. This is not, of course, in itself a principled solution, as opposed to the sceptical outlook which is, in its own way, principled. The Hobbesian solution is also notoriously unstable. A sect which could, just about, enforce conformity may be deterred by the thought of what things would be like if the other party took over. But for this to be a Hobbesian thought, as opposed to a role reversal argument which, for instance, refers to rights, some instability must be in the offing. The parties who are conscious of such a situation are likely to go in for pre-emptive strikes, and this is all the more so if the parties involved reflect that even if they can hope only for acquiescence and outer conformity in one generation, they may conceivably hope for more in later generations. As a matter of fact, in the modern world the imposition by force of political creeds and ideologies has not been very effective over time. One lesson that was already obvious in the year 1984 was the falsity in this respect of Orwell's *1984*. However, the imposition of ideology over time has certainly worked in the past, and the qualification in the previous statement, 'in the modern world', is extremely important. This is something I shall come back to.

So far, then, toleration as a *value* has barely emerged from the argument. We can have practices of toleration underlaid by scepticism or indifference, or, again, by an understood balance of power. Toleration as a value seems to demand more than this, something that can be expressed in a certain political philosophy, a certain conception of the state.

To some degree, it is possible for people to belong to communities bound together by shared convictions (religious convictions, for instance), and for toleration be sustained by a distinction between those communities and the state. The state is not identified with any set of such beliefs, and does not enforce any of them; equally, it does not allow any of the groups to impose its beliefs on the others, though each of them may of course advocate what it believes. In the United States, for instance, there is a wide consensus that supports the Constitution in allowing no law that enforces or even encourages any particular religion. There are many religious groups, and no doubt many of them have deep convictions, but none of them wants the state to suppress others, or to allow any of them to suppress others.

Many people have hoped that this can serve as a general model of the way in which a modern society can resolve the tensions of toleration. On the one hand, there are deeply held and differing convictions about moral or religious matters, held by various groups within the society. On the other hand, there is a supposedly impartial state, which affirms the rights of every citizen to equal consideration, including an equal right to form and express his or her convictions. This is the model of *liberal pluralism*. It can be seen as enacting toleration. It expresses toleration's peculiar combination of conviction and acceptance, by finding a home for people's various convictions in groups or communities less than the state, while the acceptance of diversity is located in the structure of the state itself.

This is not to say that there is no need of any shared beliefs. Clearly there must be a shared belief in the system itself. The model of a society that is held together by a framework of rights and an aspiration towards equal respect, rather than by a shared body of more specific substantive convictions, demands an ideal of citizenship that will be adequate to bear such a weight. The most impressive version of that ideal is perhaps that offered by the tradition of liberal philosophy flowing from Kant, which identifies the dignity of the human being with autonomy. A free person is one who makes his or her own life and determines his or her own convictions, and power must be used to make this possible, not to frustrate it by imposing a given set of convictions.

This is not a purely negative or sceptical ideal. If it were, it could not even hope to have the power to bind together into one society people with strongly differing convictions. Nor could it provide the motive power that all tolerant societies need in order to fight, when other means fail, the intolerant. This is an ideal associated with many contemporary liberal thinkers such as John Rawls, Thomas Nagel and Ronald Dworkin.[1]

Under the philosophy of liberal pluralism, toleration does emerge as a principled doctrine, and is represented as a value; more exactly, perhaps, it emerges as very closely related to a certain more fundamental value, that of autonomy. Because this value is taken to be understood and shared, this account of the role of toleration in liberal pluralism implies a picture of justification. It should provide an argument that could be accepted by those who do find *prima facie* intolerable outlooks that obtain in the society, and which liberalism refuses to deploy the power of the state to suppress. Thomas Nagel has expressed the matter well:

> Liberalism purports to be a view that justifies religious toleration not only to religious skeptics but to the devout, and sexual toleration not only to libertines but to those who believe extramarital sex is sinful. It distinguishes between the values a person can appeal to in conducting his own life and those he can appeal to in justifying the exercise of political power.[2]

No one, including Nagel himself, believes that this will be possible in every case. There must be, on any showing, limits to the extent to which the liberal state can be disengaged on matters of ethical disagreement. There are some questions, such as that of abortion, on which the state will fail to be neutral whatever it does. Its laws may draw distinctions between different circumstances of abortion, but in the end it cannot escape the fact that some people will believe with the deepest conviction that a certain class of acts should be permitted, while other people will believe with equal conviction that those acts should be forbidden. Equally intractable questions will arise with regard to education, where the autonomy of some fundamentalist religious groups, for instance, to bring up their children in their own beliefs will be seen by liberals as standing in conflict with the autonomy of those children to choose what beliefs they will have. No society can avoid collective and substantive choices on matters of that kind, and in that sense, on those issues, there are limits to toleration, even if people continue to respect one another's opinions.

The fact that there will be some cases that will be impossible in such a way does not necessarily wreck liberal toleration, unless there are too many of them. There is no argument of principle to show that if A thinks a certain practice is wrong and B thinks that practice is right, A has to think that the state should suppress that practice or B has to think that the state should promote that practice. These are considerations at different levels. Nevertheless, there is a famous argument to the effect that the liberal ideal is in principle impossible. Some critics of liberalism claim that the liberal pluralist state, as the supposed enactment of toleration, does not really exist. What is happening, they say, is that the state is subtly enforcing one set of principles (roughly, principles which favour individual choice, social co-operation and business efficiency) while the convictions that people previously deeply held, on matters of religion or sexual behaviour or the significance of cultural experience, dwindle into private tastes. On this showing, liberalism will be 'just another sectarian doctrine': the phrase that Rawls used precisely in explaining what liberalism had to avoid being.

What is the critic's justification for saying that the liberal state is 'subtly enforcing' one set of attitudes rather than another? Nagel distinguishes sharply between *enforcing* something like individualism, on the one hand, and the practices of liberal toleration, on the other, though he honestly and correctly admits that the educational practices, for instance, of the liberal state are not 'equal in their effects'. This is an important distinction, and it can make some significant difference in practice. It is not the same thing to be proselytised or coerced by militant individualism, and merely to see one's traditional religious surroundings eroded by a modern liberal society. The liberal's opponents must concede that there is something in the distinction, but this does not mean that they will be convinced by the use that the liberal makes of it, because it is not a distinction that is neutral in its inspiration. It is asymmetrically skewed in the liberal direction, because it makes a lot out of a difference of procedure, whereas what matters to a non-liberal believer is the difference of outcome. I doubt whether we can find an argument of principle that satisfies the purest and strongest aims of the value of liberal toleration, in the sense that it does not rely on scepticism or on the contingencies of power, and also could in principle explain to rational people whose deepest convictions were not in favour of individual autonomy and related values that they should think a state better which let their values decay in preference to enforcing them.

If toleration as a practice is to be defended in terms of its being a value, then it will have to appeal to substantive opinions about the good, in particular the good of individual autonomy, and these opinions will extend to the value and the meaning of personal characteristics and virtues associated with toleration, just as they will to the political activities of imposing or refusing to impose various substantive outlooks. This is not to say that the substantive values of individual autonomy are misguided or baseless. The point is that these values, like others, may be rejected, and to the extent that toleration rests on those values, then toleration will also be rejected. The practice of toleration cannot be based on a value such as that of individual autonomy, and also hope to escape from substantive disagreements about the good. This really is a contradiction because it is only a substantive view of goods such as autonomy that could yield the value that is expressed by the practices of toleration.

In the light of this, we can now better understand the impossibility or extreme difficulty that was seemingly presented by the personal virtue or attitude of toleration. It appeared impossible because it seemingly required someone to think that a certain belief or practice was thoroughly wrong or bad, and at the same time that there was some intrinsic good to be found in its being allowed to flourish. This does not involve a contradiction, if the other good is found not in that belief's continuing, but in the other believer's autonomy. People can coherently think that a certain outlook or attitude is deeply wrong, and that the flourishing of such an attitude should be tolerated, if they also hold another substantive value in favour of the autonomy or independence of other believers. The belief in toleration as a value, then, does not necessarily involve a contradiction, but rather that familiar thing, a conflict of goods. However, this in turn gives rise to the familiar problem that others may not share the liberal's view of those goods; in particular, the people that the liberal is particularly required to tolerate are unlikely to share the liberal's view of the good of autonomy, which is the basis of his toleration, to the extent that this expresses a value.

Granted this, it is perhaps as well that, as we saw earlier, the practice of toleration does not necessarily rest on any such value at all. It may be supported by Hobbesian considerations about what is possible or desirable in the matter of enforcement, or again by scepticism about the issues of disagreement and their eventual resolution – though with scepticism, of course, the point will be reached where nobody is sufficiently interested in the question for toleration even to be necessary. It is important, too, that these attitudes do not exist in a context in which there are no other values at all. Appeals to the misery and cruelty involved in intolerance may, in favourable circumstances, have some effect even with those who are not dedicated to toleration as an intrinsic virtue.

It may be that the best hopes for toleration are to be found not so much in the abstract principle which challenges one to combine the maximum of the pure spirit of toleration with one's detestation of what has to be tolerated. It may lie rather in modernity itself, or what is left of it, and in its principal creation, international commercial society. Despite unnerving outbreaks of fanaticism in many different directions, it is still possible to think that the structures of this international order will encourage scepticism about religious and other claims to exclusivity, and about the motives of those who impose such claims. Indeed, it can encourage such outlooks within religions themselves. When such scepticism is set against the manifest and immediate human harms generated by intolerance, there is a basis for the practice of toleration – a basis that is indeed allied to liberalism, but is less ambitious than the pure principle of liberal pluralism, which rests on autonomy. It is closer to the tradition that may be traced to Montesquieu and to Constant, which the late Judith Shklar called 'the Liberalism of Fear.'[3]

It may be that liberal societies can preserve, in an atmosphere of toleration, a variety of strong convictions on important matters. Only the future will show whether that is so, and also how much it matters to humanity whether that variety, and so all but a few convictions, will fade away. Perhaps toleration will prove to have been an interim value, serving a period between a past when no one had heard of it and a future in which no one will need it. For the present, it is very obvious that the time has not yet come when we can do without the awkward practices of toleration. But those practices have to be sustained not so much by a very pure principle as by all the resources that we can put together. Besides the belief in autonomy, those resources consist of scepticism against fanaticism and the pretensions of its advocates; conviction about the manifest evils of toleration's absence; and, quite certainly, power.

Notes

1. See John Rawls, *A Theory of Justice,* Oxford, Oxford University Press, 1971; John Rawls, *Political Liberalism,* Columbia, Columbia University Press, 1993; Thomas Nagel, *Equality and Impartiality,* Oxford, Oxford University Press, 1991; Ronald Dworkin, 'What is Equality?', *Philosophy and Public Affairs,* 10, 1981.
2. Nagel, *Equality and Impartiality*, p. 156.
3. Judith Shklar, 'The Liberalism of Fear' in Nancy Rosenblum (ed.), *Liberalism and the Moral Life*, Cambridge, Mass., Harvard University Press, 1989, pp. 21–38.

Chapter 6

Nationalism and toleration
Michael Ignatieff

I

In 1917, in the course of an essay on 'The Taboo of Virginity', Freud observed in passing that 'it is precisely the minor differences in people who are otherwise alike that form the basis of feelings of strangeness and hostility between them'. He went on, 'it would be tempting to pursue this idea and to derive from this "narcissism of minor differences" the hostility which in every human relation we see fighting against feelings of fellowship and overpowering the commandment that all men should love one another'.[1]

Freud is illuminating a paradox at the root of the psychology of intolerance: that it is not the common elements humans share with each other which organise their perception of their own identities, but the marginal 'minor' elements which divide them. In the first instance, Freud had in mind gender difference. Men and women share the same genetic endowment, down to a chromosome or two, yet when deriving their sense of identity, they focus exclusively on the minor sexual differences between them. What Marx called 'species being' – our identity as members of the same species – counts for relatively little in the formation of our self-image. Male identity, for example, does not begin from a perception of our essential similarity with females. This in itself is not surprising since all identities are formed by differentiation, by establishing the salience of a difference. What is puzzling is that this differentiation process should be accompanied by such large amounts of anxiety. Why is it that men's identities depend on the constitution of woman as an object, not merely of desire, but fear? 'Perhaps this dread is based on the fact that woman is different from man, for ever incomprehensible and mysterious, strange and therefore apparently hostile. The man is afraid of being weakened by the woman, infected with her femininity and of then showing himself incapable.' Strange, and therefore hostile. Why is it that minor difference should be strange, *and therefore* hostile? Why is it that, sharing so much, we humans should fear our minor differences so intensely?

When Freud returned to the 'narcissism of minor differences' five years later, in 'Group Psychology and the Analysis of the Ego', the focus of his analysis had shifted from the differences between men and women to the antagonisms dividing social groups. Even in intimate groups – 'friendship, marriage, the relations between parents and children' – emotions of hostility and suspicion competed with feelings of human kinship. Here too 'species identity' and even long-standing emotional bonds are never sufficient to overcome feelings of hostility entirely. The emotional result is ambivalence, and it arises, not, Freud thinks, primarily because of conflicts of interest, but because of the intrinsically antipathetic and aggressive character of all identity formation. Both in the family and in larger social and political units, Freud argued, the closer the relation between human beings the more hostile they were likely to be towards each other:

> Of two neighbouring towns each is the other's most jealous rival; every little canton looks down upon the others with contempt. Closely related races keep one another at arm's length; the South German cannot endure the North German, the Englishman casts every kind of aspersion upon the Scot, the Spaniard despises the Portuguese. We are no longer astonished that greater differences should lead to an almost insuperable repugnance, such as the Gallic people feel for the German, the Aryan for the Semite and the white races for the coloured.[2]

As he widens his analysis out to include national and racial difference, Freud seems to muddy the distinction between major and minor difference. Why should sexual difference between men and women be minor, while racial difference be major? For the moment, let us leave this difficulty aside and observe the paradox which Freud wishes us to notice: that the level of hostility and intolerance between groups bears no relation to the objective character of the differences between them. Indeed, the smaller the real difference between groups, the larger it will loom in their mutual self-definitions. He then goes on to suggest that such hostility is connected to 'narcissism':

> In the undisguised antipathies and aversion which people feel towards strangers with whom they have to do we may recognize the expression of self-love – or narcissism. This self-love works for the preservation of the individual, and behaves as though the occurrence of any divergence from his own particular lines of development involved a criticism of them and a demand for their alteration.

The facts of difference themselves are neutral. It is the narcissist who turns them into a judgement upon himself. Narcissist anxiety expresses itself chiefly in passive self-absorption and epistemological closure. A narcissist is uncurious about others except to the extent that they reflect back upon himself. What is different is rejected if it fails to confirm the narcissist in his or her own self-opinion.

Freud does not explain why some forms of narcissism are essentially passive, others more aggressive. In the original Greek myth, after all, Narcissus is an archetype of passive self-absorption. He stares at his own reflection, oblivious to the world. Freud does not explain why it is that the same self-absorbed figure can suddenly come awake from his daze of self-love and attack those who break into his reverie. But in connecting self-absorption to a capacity for aggression, Freud does help us to detect an unseen connection between the aggressive forms of narcissism and intolerance. One observable characteristic of intolerant people is that they are actively uninterested in learning about those they purport to despise. Freud helps us to see this form of closure as a narcissistic defence of their own identities. On this reading, intolerance is a closed system, a self-referential circuit in which a narcissist uses the external world only to reproduce confirmation of his essential beliefs. It is the narcissistic investment in intolerant belief which makes it so uniquely unresponsive to rational argument.

Likewise, and once again by extrapolating a little from Freud, it becomes possible to think of nationalism as a kind of narcissism. A nationalist takes the neutral facts about a people – their language, habitat, culture, tradition and history – and turns these facts into a narrative, whose purpose is to illuminate the self-consciousness of a group, to enable them to think of themselves as a nation, with a claim to self-determination. A nationalist, in other words, takes 'minor differences', – indifferent in themselves – and transforms them into major differences, turns them into a mirror in which people suddenly see themselves as having a destiny and a vocation. For this purpose, traditions are invented, a glorious past is gilded and refurbished for public consumption, and a people who might not have thought of themselves as a people at all suddenly begin to dream of themselves as a nation. What is interesting about seeing nationalism as a kind of narcissism is that it enables us to focus on the projective and self-regarding quality of the nationalistic discourse. Nationalism is a distorting mirror in which believers see their simple ethnic, religious or territorial attributes transformed into glorious attributes and qualities. Though Freud does not explain exactly how this happens, the systematic over-valuation of the self results in systematic devaluation of strangers and outsiders. In this way narcissistic self-regard depends upon and in turn exacerbates intolerance.

Freud himself returned to the connection between narcissism and intolerance in his essay 'Civilization and its Discontents', written in 1929. There he observes that 'it is always possible to bind together a considerable number of people in love, so long as there are other people left over to receive the manifestations of their aggressiveness'. A narcissistic group maintains its cohesion by displacing its aggression and hostility outwards. It does so with a clean conscience because its narcissism enables it to regard the other group in purely negative terms, as an instance of everything the group does not wish itself to be. He then goes on to observe sardonically that his own people, the Jews, have 'rendered the most useful services to the civilizations of the countries that have been their hosts', by providing them with a convenient target for all their suppressed hostilities. Freud locates the essential source of this hostility in the psychological implausibility of Christianity as a religion of love: 'When once the Apostle Paul had posited universal love between men as the foundation of his Christian community, extreme intolerance on the part of

Christendom towards those who remained outside it became the inevitable consequence.'[3] Christianity, in Freud's reading, is a paradigmatic kind of collective narcissism. It envelops believers in the fiction that theirs is a community of love. But the maintenance of such a fiction requires repression of the essential aggressiveness in all human beings, with the result that the Christian self-image can only be preserved by diverting hate outwards to a people who are then designated, despite all the other available identities they present, as the killers of Christ.

Let us pause here and draw some implications from what Freud is arguing. If intolerance and narcissism are connected, one immediate and practical conclusion might seem to be: we are only likely to love others more if we also learn to love ourselves a little less. Breaking down stereotypical images of others is only likely to work if we also break down the fantastic elements in our own self-regard. The root of intolerance seems to be found in our tendency to over-value ourselves.

How can we correct this without falling into excessive self-abasement? Presumably by learning to look on ourselves with a cold eye, to see ourselves as others see us, and to awaken from the protective cocoon of our narcissism. Freud's therapeutic process – the talking cure – was conceived as a struggle to emancipate oneself from deluded self-images by a process of self-distancing, by standing apart and seeing ourselves through the eyes of others. Such an ideal is difficult enough for individuals to practise. Is such a 'talking cure' conceivable for groups, or for nations? Actually, the idea is not as far-fetched as it might seem, but one does have to imagine a country having a conversation with itself, in a million competing voices. It is just possible that such a conversation occurred in West Germany after the Second World War, a talking through of the relation between nationalism and intolerance which left most, though not all, members of society thinking and behaving differently after the conversation had been concluded.

Freud's remarks about narcissism and intolerance were written on the eve of Hitler's coming to power. The following decade saw Freud himself and his family driven into exile. It cannot be accidental that an Austrian Jew should have had such deep intuitions about narcissism and minor difference. No group was prouder to be German than the Jews; no national minority was more successfully assimilated. Freud himself, just like Heine before him, wrote the German language with particular skill and beauty. He combined a proud consciousness of being Jewish, indeed of following in the rabbinical tradition of law–giver and seer, with a deep attachment to German classical culture and the tastes and habits of the South German bourgeoisie.

None of this saved Freud or Austrian Jewry. No matter how assiduously they assimilated, no matter how carefully they eliminated the differences that separated them from their fellow Germans, the simple fact of being Jewish remained; that simple, surely minor fact (minor, that is, to many Jews for whom it was a vestigial identity, one among many), Hitler turned into a major 'biological' gulf between two races and cultures. The narcissism of minor difference thus describes, if it does not explain, the irony that nations where Jews were thoroughly assimilated showed themselves to be as anti-Semitic as those, like Poland, where they were not. As assimilation eliminated major elements of difference, minor vestiges acquired an increasingly neurotic salience among those, like Hitler, whose identities were threatened by Jewish assimilation. Hitler succeeded in redescribing assimilation as a pollution; once this was done, reasserting the absolute gulf between the Aryan and the Jew was easily conceived as an act of purification. This language of purity and cleansing, so full of echoes today, is perhaps the most elemental of all languages of narcissism: the reduction of all difference to the distinction between cleanliness and dirt. Cleanliness becomes the distinction between the human and the non-human, between the valued and the despised. This is the trajectory, the path towards moral abjection, to which the narcissism of minor difference can (though it need not always) lead.

It is at this point that we should return to a central difficulty in Freud's analysis, namely which differences count as major, which as minor. Freud himself appears to imbibe the fantasies of his own time, to the effect that racial difference is major, while breaking with his time in maintaining that gender differences were minor. Yet in the light of the substantial elements which all humans share with each other, it could be said that all human difference is minor, or more precisely, pales in significance beside the elements which we share.

One could go on to argue, in fact, that the differences which matter are those between individuals within groups, and not between the groups themselves. Genetic research seems to show that there are no significant variations in the distribution of intelligence, cognitive or moral ability between racial, ethnic or gender-based groups, but there are significant variations among individuals within these groups.

Intolerance customarily fixes on the group differences as the ones that are salient and tends to ignore the differences between individuals in the loathed group. Indeed, in most forms of intolerance, the individuality of the person who is despised is all but ignored; what counts is merely his or her membership in the group. As I said earlier, intolerant people are fundamentally uncurious, uninterested in the groups they despise except in so far as their behaviour confirms their prejudices. Going further, one could say that intolerant people are uninterested in the individuals who compose despised groups: indeed they hardly see 'them' as individuals at all. What matters is the constitution of a primal opposition between 'them' and 'us'. Individuality only complicates the picture, indeed makes prejudice more difficult to sustain, since it is at the individual level that forms of identification and affection can arise to subvert the primal opposition of 'them' and 'us'. Intolerance, on this analysis, is a willed refusal to focus on individual difference, and a perverse insistence that individual identity is subsumed in the group. The difference between individual and group is major; the difference between groups is minor – yet perversely, intolerance focuses on the latter, rather than upon the former.

It is worth speculating that if intolerant groups are unable or unwilling to perceive those they despise as individuals, it is because intolerant individuals are unable or unwilling to perceive themselves as such either. Their own identities are too insecure to permit individuation: they cannot see themselves as the makers of their individualities and hence they cannot see others as makers of theirs either. In their intolerance, they allow themselves to be spoken for by the collective discourses that have taken them over; they do not, as it were, speak in their own right. On this account, the narcissism of minor difference is a leap into collective fantasy which enables threatened or anxious individuals to avoid the burden of thinking for themselves or even of thinking of themselves as individuals. Why these identities should be so vulnerable will depend on who they are and what threatens them. Later, in discussing nationalism in more specific historic contexts, I will try to explain why certain national groups feel more threatened in their identity than others and therefore more vulnerable to the fantasies of narcissism. For the moment what should be observed is that the practice of toleration depends, critically, on being able to individualise oneself and others, to be able to 'see' oneself and others in our singularity, or to put it another way, to be able to focus on 'major' difference – which is individual – and not on 'minor' difference – which is collective.

II

I now want to illuminate these general considerations with some practical examples, drawn from the world of modern nationalism. In particular, I want to distinguish between the types of nationalism and their relation to intolerance. It is a truism to say that nationalism leads necessarily to intolerance. Like all truisms, this one is not necessarily true: some stridently nationalistic societies – America, for example – are not obviously more intolerant than more quietly nationalistic ones, like Britain. It all depends on the type of nationalism and the type of society. I want to illuminate the relationship between nationalism and intolerance by asking which particular kinds of nationalism, in which particular situations, are most likely to breed intolerance. Or to put the same question in another way, why it is that certain forms of intensely nationalistic society find the practice of tolerance towards neighbouring ethnic societies or ethnic minorities within their own society not merely difficult, but actually repugnant?

The kind of intolerance I am interested in is the kind which is directed not against beliefs, doctrines, practices or actions, but against the very fact of difference – in this case, against ethnic difference itself. This is not the intolerance against which the classical texts of the liberal tradition were directed. Locke was writing against intolerance towards specific doctrine and belief, maintaining that it was strictly irrational to compel individuals to abandon propositions they believed to be true, since the psychic state of being persuaded of propositions does not and cannot depend on the will. 'Such is the nature of the understanding that it cannot be compelled to the belief of anything by outward force.'[4] The intolerance in which I am interested is not directed at what people believe, but towards who they are, that is, to the totality of those signs (skin colour, religion, language, dietary customs, dress and behaviour) which demarcate them as different, and which, crucially, are also not subject to their individual wills. Such intolerance, it should be noted, shares the irrationality which Locke identified in relation to those forms of intolerance directed at belief. Individuals are blamed and condemned for being something which is not in their power to alter. (Intolerant individuals do not treat those they despise as individuals, except in one respect: they argue as if each was to blame for what they are. Difference is perceived as a group matter; but guilt continues to be attributed individually.)

If tolerance means 'live and let live', the intolerance I am interested in is one which claims that it is impossible and undesirable for different ethnic groups to 'live and let live', that is, to share the same state, territory and resources; the intolerance which insists on the necessity and the right of each ethnic group to follow what the South African apartheid regime used to call 'separate development'. This is an intolerance expressed in terms of an extreme moral and cultural relativism. It insists that group identities are so all-shaping that they create moral worlds unintelligible to each other, and that groups therefore are incapable of living together in peace within the same territorial and political space. This form of intolerance underpins ethnic cleansing in Bosnia, Christian–Muslim conflict in the south Caucasus, Afrikaner claims to separate homelands for whites in South Africa and perhaps also so-called tribal warfare in Rwanda. This intolerance often tacitly presumes the superiority of a particular group, but it is more often relativist and separatist; it may only insist on the impossibility of sharing civic space with other groups.

One might have expected such intolerance to be most prevalent where two ethnic groups differ most, in terms of language, religion, culture or style of life. The narcissism of minor difference makes us realise that the opposite is just as likely. In Bosnia, for example, there are three groups – Muslim, Croat and Serb – who have come, over the past three generations, to resemble each other so closely that it cannot be said that they are ethnically distinct at all. Yet all are actively engaged in the late twentieth century's most odious, certainly most publicised form of intolerance – ethnic cleansing. My question is why ethnic cleansing appears where it does, and what role nationalist beliefs play in making ethnic cleansing possible. It is a truism to say that ethnic cleansing is a 'result' of nationalism. I want to explain in what sense this truism is true.

In popular parlance nationalism has almost become a synonym for intolerance; at the very least, nationalism is seen as an intolerant form of patriotism. The distinction between patriotism and nationalism is not easy to draw: one person's patriotism is another's nationalism. We often call societies nationalistic, when all we mean is that they are intensely patriotic. I did so earlier in contrasting the intense nationalism of America with the quieter, less obvious, nationalism of Britain. In principle at least the two are distinguishable. Patriotism is love of a country one can take for granted as one's own; it is love for a country whose borders are settled, whose identity is more or less secure, and which does not have large groups of its own people subject to the domination or control of another country. The intense love of country one meets with in the United States, or occasionally in Britain in time of war, is more properly called patriotism than nationalism. As an uncontested emotion, patriotism can be, though it is not always, free of intolerant aggression towards other nations or peoples.

Nationalism, typically, is love of a country that happens to belong to someone else. Nationalists frequently belong to nations that do not have a state of their own; either because they are ruled by some colonial or imperial power, or because they are a subjugated national minority in the state of another national group. Nationalism, by definition, is a contested claim to self-determination, and because it is contested, it is often a source of conflict and intolerance. It arises, typically, where ethnic difference has been overlaid with domination, that is to say, where one group has ruled another, where ethnicity has conferred political, economic, or cultural authority over another. It is a history of domination, characteristically, which turns the simple facts of ethnic difference into an abyss of narcissism in the dominant group and wounded pride and resentment on the part of the dominated group.

Although popular usage treats nationalism as a set of emotions, it is in fact a political doctrine with three essential components: that the peoples of the world naturally divide into nations; that these nations should have the right to rule themselves; and that this exercise in self-determination should, in most cases, result in each nation having a sovereign state of its own. Since there are several thousand groups of people who call themselves nations, and under two hundred re-cognised states, the number of unmet nationalist claims, and therefore potential sources of conflict and intolerance in the world, is very large.

There are herbivore and carnivore nationalisms: nationalisms whose chief manifestation is love of one's own, and those where love of one's own seems inseparable from hatred of others; those nationalisms which are linked to intolerance and those which are not. In *Blood and Belonging*, I connect these distinctions to two basic criteria according to which nations define who belongs, the civic or the ethnic.[5] Civic nationalism – of the French, British and American type – defines the nation, not in terms of birth or ethnicity, but in terms of willingness to adhere to its civic values. Allegiance is essentially directed towards the state and its civic institutions and values. Ethnic nationalism – of the German and Polish type – defines the nation in terms of ethnic origins and birth. Allegiance is directed primarily at the nation, at the traditions, values and cultures incar-nated in a people's history.

In societies of a civic nationalist type, belonging is not tied to birth or ethnic origin, yet forms of national patriotic sentiment – French and American republicanism being the most successful examples – can be extremely strong. Indeed, in the American case, the more heterogeneous the ethnic composition of the republic, the more insistently patriotic its discourse becomes, or rather, the more central to that discourse becomes the claim that the nation state is capable of giving a home and a welcome to all. Civic nationalist societies are not always tolerant places: the patriotic consensus can become so overbearing that the right to differ may be over-run; and when demagogues succeed in convincing people that the country is in danger, as Senator McCarthy did in the 1950s, patriotism easily turns into paranoia. Yet – and this anticipates my argument – a society anchored in a culture of individual rights and liberties is more easily returned to the practice of toleration than one where social allegiance is invested in ethnicity.

Societies premised on an ethnic nationalist criterion of belonging have a different record in relation to tolerance of ethnic difference, and it is these ethnic nationalist societies that I want to look at. Not all ethnically homogeneous states are intolerant: the Finns, Hungarians, Norwegians, Swedes and Czechs are more or less ethnically unified, and yet do not appear substantially intolerant societies. But in some societies, like the German, there has been a strong historical connection between anti-Semitic intolerance and the definition of nationality by *jus sanguinis*, by birth and Germanity, rather by residence and choice. Polish anti-Semitism, likewise, may owe much to the essentially ethnico-religious basis of Polish national sentiment. Thus it may not be ethnic homogeneity or an ethnic basis for citizenship alone which create conditions for intolerance. Additional historical experiences of national humiliation may be necessary to turn ethnic consciousness into ethnic paranoia: in the Polish case, the humiliation of an extinguished statehood, from the eighteenth-century partitions to the treaty of Versailles; in the German case, war-time defeat, an onerous peace settlement, recent and therefore insecure national unification coupled with a particularly messianic and universalising conception of German cultural mission.

The Polish–German comparison is instructive: intensely self-aggrandising and narcissistic national cultures, whose identity is based on *jus sanguinis*, lacking the continuity and security of stable state structures, and recovering from a traumatic national defeat. Experience suggests that these are the conditions which produce the intolerant nationalisms.

Serbia offers another example of the same pattern. An ethnically homogeneous nation with a proud, self-aggrandising history, but an historically weak state, the Serbs are intensely conscious of themselves as the historical leader of the Balkan peoples: going down to glorious defeat against the Turks in Kosova Field in 1389, and then becoming the first people in the Ottoman empire to wage a successful nation-alist struggle of liberation between 1819 and 1859. This made them the Piedmontese of the Balkans, the people who took upon them-selves the historical task of unifying the South Slavs and freeing them from the Ottoman and Austro-Hungarian yokes. The Serbs think of themselves as the warrior defenders of the border reaches of Eur-opean Christendom against the Muslim foe. Yet they are a numeri-cally small people, struggling for statehood in a region which historically has been the major point of intersection and conflict between the Christian and Islamic empires in Europe. A nationalism forged in the crucible of imperial conflict must necessarily have memories of humiliation and defeat, from Kosova in 1389 to the heroic but catastrophic winter retreat of the Serbian armies into Montenegro and Albania in 1915. Serbia is a case of a small nation with grandiose dreams which it is not strong enough to realise – chief among these dreams being the reunification of all Serbs within one contiguous territorial state. Serbia is also a case of a small nation which feels it has fought for Europe, on its border marches with the Islamic world, but which has never been rewarded or acknowledged by Europe for its sacrifices. Yet as it longs for European recognition, it also doubts whether it actually belongs to Europe. As an Eastern Orthodox people, it feels, like the Russians, that its very belonging to Europe is in question. Is it of the East or of the West? These uncertainties and weaknesses in its identity as a nation leave it especially vulnerable to paranoia and to intolerance, leave its popu-lace vulnerable to a demagoguery which insists that nobody under-stands them but themselves. This form of 'epistemological closure' may be a common feature of 'intolerant' nationalisms, by which I mean a conviction that their history locks them into a situation which can only be understood from the inside, never from the outside; that all outsiders, especially those from the Great Powers, who have so often presided over or witnessed their humiliation, can never be true or reliable friends.

Croatian nationalism shares similar characteristics with the Serbs: Croats think of themselves as a small people with a great vocation, a frontier people, at the border between East and West, Christianity and Islam, a colonised people whose great dreams of nationhood have been continually frustrated by outside powers. Yet while Serbs have gloried in fighting alone for statehood, Croats have always collaborated with outside powers to attain their nationalist designs. They quarried out a domain of autonomy within the Austro-Hungarian empire; and then, less defensibly, aligned themselves with the fascist occupiers in the Second World War to create their own independent state. It is central to Croatian nationalist consciousness to believe that they belong to Western Catholic European civilisation, while Serbs are Orthodox, Eastern, 'Balkan' in all that is pejorative in the term.

It is worth enlarging on the narcissistic role of the concept of 'Europe' in nationalist consciousness. The slogan which all the societies of Eastern Europe took to using as they exited from the Communist era was that they were 'returning to Europe'. By this they meant a return to the European values of toleration, freedom and democracy, abandoned or betrayed by the Communist experiment; a return to the European capitalist market; and prospectively at least, insertion in the 'European' community. Because these societies had always been European, the return to Europe meant integration in *Western* Europe. This 'return' has proved difficult, not least because Western Europe, for all its high-flown talk about a continent stretching from Liverpool to Vladivostok, in its heart of hearts believed Europe actually ended at the Oder–Neisse line.

Usually the terms 'Europe' and 'nationalism' are seen as antitheses. Europe stands for the values of a civilisation, chief among them being tolerance, which transcend national division. In reality, 'Europe' figures constantly within nationalist consciousness as a neuralgic element of national pride, resentment, and above all, self-differentiation with other neighbours held to be 'less' European. Thus Croats think of themselves as 'better' Europeans than Serbs; Serbs bitterly resent that they are not considered 'good Europeans'. In Western Europe, too, there remains a strongly competitive element in each nation's attempt to wrest the definition of European values for itself. Moreover, Eastern Europeans mean something very different by the term 'European' to Western Europeans. Thus both Serbs and Croats use 'European' as a synonym for 'non-Muslim', a usage which has impeccable historical credentials, but ones which most West

Europeans had forgotten, at least that is, until the Iranian Revolution and the Rushdie affair. Given that Europe is supposed to stand for tolerant supra-nationalism, it is ironic, and also depressing, that the competition to be thought more 'European' than one's neighbours is a central source of intolerant nationalist emotion right across the continent.

As a matter of historical fact, Europe does not 'stand' for toleration, any more than it stands for 'ethnic cleansing'. The doctrine of toleration *is* a European invention, but so is the concentration camp. Since the religious massacres of the Reformation and Counter-Reformation, ethnic or at least confessional cleansing has been as central an element of European behaviour as the practices of toleration and the doctrine of universal human rights. Yet the Europe which all of these post-Communist states are rushing to join is all too frequently conceived, imaginatively, as a history-free Disneyland of tolerance, decency and 'live and let live'.

As for toleration, if it is a specifically Western European value, it arose in specific historical circumstances which are not easily replicated. It can be seen as the answer produced by seventeenth-century jurists, philosophers and statesmen to the question created by the Reformation and the break-up of the unity of Christendom in the sixteenth century: how to ensure civil peace within societies that do not have confessional uniformity. This break-up of Christendom gave enormous impetus to the philosophical attempt to understand how society itself cohered. If everyone no longer believed the same things, how did such organisms hold together? From Hobbes, through Locke and Adam Smith, the theory of society as an order of free, contracting individuals uniting together to guarantee each other security, liberty and prosperity began to take shape. This attempt to theorise social order in individualistic terms meant doing away with the premise of ethnic and confessional homogeneity as the principle of social coherence. Toleration emerges as a doctrine, therefore, within the context of a reconceptualisation of society itself, as an organism bound together, not by ties of birth and ascription, be they ethnic or confessional, but by the new ties of interest, property and rights. In this sense, toleration as doctrine, practice and habit of mind emerges with and in turn presumes a society of free, contractual individuals.

What practical implications follow from this historical point? It might just be that toleration depends on a civic order in which the rights of the individual are held to be prior to and constitutive of the social order. It cannot function in 'organicist' societies, where the social order is prior to and constitutive of individual rights. This may be the 'European' invention of which we are so proud, and the question arises whether toleration can sink roots in societies which do not have rights-based, individualistic cultures like our own. The point is not that toleration is alien to Eastern Europe, or that it is futile to insist on human rights standards in such societies. The problem is that before you can have tolerance, as a social practice, you have to create a political culture in which human identity itself is seen as individual and civic, rather than ethnic and collective. Transition to democratic regimes can occur almost overnight. The transition to a tolerant culture, tragically, requires time, peace and prosperity, and all three are in short supply in Eastern Europe.

III

Let us return to the theme of the narcissism of minor difference and observe what it illuminates about ethnic conflict around the world.

If both Serbian and Croatian nationalism belong to that particular category of intolerant nationalisms – that is, nationalisms with a strong ethnic component mixed in with memories of humiliation and defeat – what still has to be explained is why they should become enemies of each other. Why, in other words, should such extreme intolerance arise between two peoples who share so much, including a common language? From 1918 to 1989, Serbs and Croats spoke a language called Serbo-Croatian. In dialect, pronunciation, vocabulary and orthography, there were differences in how each group used the language, but these differences were minor. Since 1989, nationalists on both sides have insisted that there is a Serbian language, in a Cyrillic alphabet with a distinctive vocabulary and pronunciation, and Croat nationalists for their part are busy purifying the Croatian language of apparently foreign or Orthodox Slavic impurities. Here is a classic example of the processes of narcissism magnifying a minor difference into a major one.

But it might be argued that the differences between the two sides actually are quite significant. It is certainly true that the Croatian culture is Catholic in origin, whereas the Serb is Orthodox, and that these two peoples live on the historic frontier between Western European Catholicism and Eastern Orthodoxy. Samuel Huntingdon and others have seen nationalist conflict as a sub-set of a much larger and more elemental encounter between opposing civilisations: Muslim, Catholic and Orthodox. Yet this ignores the fact that confessional observance has waned on all sides of the battle-front, so that for the vast majority of the population religion had become a merely nominal rather than a real marker of identity. Substantial intermarriage has further blurred the confessional markers. Yet as war enveloped the Slavonian plains in 1991, fighters on each side took to wearing Orthodox and Catholic crosses, although few of these young men could have been in their respective churches since baptism. Here is a case where narcissism leads the two groups to reinvent differences that had all but disappeared.

In addition, these processes are occurring in a society which since 1960 has been undergoing rapid modernisation. Serbs, Muslims and Croats all benefited from the development that occurred in Tito's Yugoslavia in the 1960s, and which for a time made the country the most prosperous and free in the Communist world. Both Serbs and Croats had the opportunity, in their millions, to work as *gastarbeiter* in Northern Europe, and both were able to return, with their incomes and their Mercedes, and construct nearly identical villas. A substantial convergence in the lifestyles and aspirations of ethnic groups has occurred over the past thirty years, yet it is precisely here that the most violent ethnic warfare in Europe has exploded. It is these Mercedes and these villas which both sides share, and which both sides are so intent to destroy. In other words, modernisation and a convergence of forms and styles of life to a Western European model have done nothing to abate, indeed may have exacerbated, ethnic conflict. Thus, it might even be true that when ethnicity was genuinely primitive, backward, 'tribal' and rooted in local Balkan village life, it was relatively peaceful. As it has become modern, open to the world of modern media, travel, exposure to the outside world, it has become murderous. How are we to explain these paradoxes? Is nationalist intolerance a reaction against the convergences and homogenisation represented by modernisation? That is certainly Ernest Gellner's account of nationalism.[6] Instead of seeing nationalism as an atavistic resurgence of the primordial and tribal, he interprets it as a fundamentally modern attempt to reinvent forms of community and belonging and identity in the face of the loss of traditional expressions of these values in the course of modernisation. But if this is so, how exactly does it happen? Why is it that the opening to the world represented by modernisation seems only to produce the closure of ethnic particularism and conflict?

Two elements proved fatal in the Balkan case. The first was the very nature of the narcissist fantasy to which the Serbian and Croatian political elite succumbed: the idea that state and nation could coincide in one contiguous territory. This was a fantasy for the simple reason that one third of the Serb population lives outside the border of Serbia; and a substantial proportion of the Croatian population lives beyond Croatia. National unification, or the fusing of state and nation, could only occur at the cost of substantial territorial aggrandisement and ethnic cleansing. That is to say, the nationalist fantasy violently contradicted the objective realities of the Balkans. Again, one can only explain the inability of the actors to see what was staring them in the face if one gives due emphasis to nationalism as a form or narcissism, as a self-image so alluring that, as in the fable of Narcissus itself, it lures those who fall for it to their deaths.

The second crucial element was the collapse of the Titoist state. Mutual toleration between ethnic groups is always possible provided there is an overarching state which, both nominally and practically, affords all equal protection before the law, or to put it another way, protects each ethnic group against the other. In a situation like the Balkans where, over substantial areas like Bosnia, no one ethnic group has an overwhelming demographic advantage (in other words where all groups are more or less equally powerful minorities) a super-ordinate state is the very condition of mutual toleration. In the Yugoslav case, however, the post-war state was built on two pillars, both made of sand: one-party hegemony, and the personal charisma of a dictator. When these two pillars collapsed, as they were bound to do, ethnic groups were then delivered into the Hobbesian war of all against all. In this situation, it ceased to be rational for individuals to practise the forms of inter-ethnic accommodation and tolerance which had grown up under the aegis of the Titoist state. As demagogues began to mobilise the population on nationalist lines, as the state order began to fragment, it became rational, instead, for individuals to look to their group for protection. As they did so, the seductions of narcissistic identification became harder to resist. But we should not forget that if they ended up imprisoned inside ethnic narcissism, they were driven there, fundamentally, by the collapse of the state, and by the fear and terror which followed. The central point is that, as individuals, Serbs and Croats were only too aware that it was deeply irrational, in a society of densely interwoven ethnic accommodation and intermarriage, for each ethnic group to look to their own for protection. As individuals, they knew it was far better to live with each other in peace. But once the state collapsed, once there was no institution capable of providing protection for all, toleration ceased to be a rational strategy; instead everyone ran to the protection of their own.

The essential dynamic in the Yugoslav case is quite specific to the Balkans, to the extremely diffuse and splintered patterns of ethnic settlement in the region and to the Hobbesian conflict likely to break out there once state authority disintegrated. Yet many key elements in the Yugoslav case, notably the way in which modernisation heightens the narcissism of minor difference, can be observed throughout the world.

In Turkey, for example, an authoritarian secular state has devoted seventy years to extirpating – by force – the difference between Kurds and Turks. These two peoples may appear to outsiders to be nearly indistinguishable: most Turkish Kurds, for example, only speak Turkish. Yet the forcible modernisation and integration of Turkey has only exacerbated the conflict between the two peoples, so that now southern Turkey is a war-zone, a battle-ground between the intolerant, unitary nationalism of Kemal Ataturk and the in-surgent populist nationalism of the Kurdish PKK.

Similarly, in Israel, it is striking how much hostility there is between Sephardi Jews and Arabs, even though an outsider sitting at the tables of both might notice a remarkable similarity in certain foods, attitudes towards male authority, presence of the female in the household. Some of the most intransigent members of the right-wing Israeli parties are composed of Yemeni Jews, who seem to an outsider to be as Semitic as their Arab enemies. Paradoxically, it is Jews of European origin, who often have very little in common with the Middle Eastern ethos shared by both Arabs and Sephardim alike, who often, though not invariably, seem most inclined towards the rule of toleration and peace in relation to the Arab and Palestinian community.

Ukraine, likewise, illustrates the same theme: that as modernisation reduces the salient differences between ethnic groups, nationalism emerges to inflame the minor differences that remain. In Ukraine, ethnic Russians and Ukrainians appear to share common linguistic, cultural and religious elements, and where they differ, they differ at the margins: Ukrainian Uniate Catholicism can be considered a variety of Orthodoxy; just as the Ukrainian language can be considered a variant, though a significant variant, of Russian. In the Soviet period, moreover, both Russians and Ukrainians were hammered together by the combined weight of Soviet power, artificially created famine and the suppression of nationalist difference in the name of socialist brotherhood and unity. The net effect, paradoxically, is that as the Communist yoke collapsed, nationalist consciousness, far from being eroded over the previous seventy-five years of enforced Stalinist modernisation, came back more strongly than ever. Now, as economic catastrophe stares both ethnic Ukrainians and ethnic Russians in the face – in other words, as the economics of their common plight suggests the necessity of co-operation – there are elements on both sides driving their peoples towards civil war within Ukraine. How can this be happening when both peoples have sound historical reasons to consider themselves 'brothers'?

Indeed, as the reference to brothers suggests, it may be that the appropriate title for the paradox I am exploring is 'The Cain and Abel Syndrome': the ironic fact that intolerance between brothers is often stronger than that between strangers. The analytical question, therefore, is how the essential elements of similarity which make groups 'brothers' are denied and reconstrued so that the two groups confront each other as 'strangers'.

This same syndrome can be illustrated in Northern Ireland, where what has to be explained is why patterns of intolerance, inherited from a religious era, should have been exacerbated, rather than reduced, as both communities modernise and secular-ise. The Troubles are presented as an ethno-religious conflict, yet neither the ethnic nor the religious elements in the identity of each side are unambiguous markers of difference. Attempts are made, on the Catholic side, to construe the Protestants as an alien group, as settlers, colonists of Scottish or English ethnic origin; on the Protestant side, attempts are made to construe the Catholics as equally alien, 'bog Irish' primitives, tied to such un-British super-stitions as the doctrine of papal supremacy. In reality, both sides have lived on the same spot for more than three hundred years; there are substantial tendencies to intermarriage, just as there are in the Serb and Croat cases. The reality is that both Ulstermen and Republicans have equal claims to calling themselves Irish. As in the Serb and Croat cases, though to a markedly smaller degree, confessional observance is declining and religion functions as a community marker, rather than as a lived element of identity. As responsible figures on both sides never tire of saying, though to little effect, the confessional differences between Protestantism and Catholicism cannot obscure the fact that both religions preach tolerance as both a private and a public virtue. Both sides, more-over, inhabit a substantially disadvantaged region, and one might have expected that common economic hardship might create shared bonds of class or economic interest. Finally, the substantial elements of disadvantage in the Catholic community – second-class housing, job discrimination, police harassment – are less salient as causes of discontent and as a marker of difference than they were. And yet, despite all the elements which ought to bring the two sides together – declining confessional observance, shared economic hardship – the conflict, if anything, has hardened the two communities' identities into frozen masks of uncompromising intolerance. Yet, as the two antagonists frequently admit, no one understands the other as well as they do: they are truly brother enemies; and an outsider who cannot tell a Protestant and a Catholic apart, from accent, dress or deportment, will soon become aware that each side has developed an extraordinarily elaborate code, relating to personal names, place of residence, modes of transport, favourite pubs, and so on, to figure out who is actually who. What appears to be happening is a fanatically ingenious, creative and elaborate attempt by elements within the two communities to deny the common humanity on which a regime of mutual tolerance might be erected.

   A more peaceful example of the same paradox about identity and difference can be observed in my native country, Canada. French and English Canadian communities have shared the same state for one hundred and twenty-five years; both communities are deeply shaped by the experience of English common law and the heritage of British colonial administration; both share a common life in the same deeply inhospitable climate; both enjoy many of the same pastimes, chief among them, hockey. In many respects, the pattern of life in both communities is more similar than it was three generations ago when Quebec was indeed one of the more backward regions of North America. Then it was a rural society, much poorer than the rest of English Canada, heavily controlled by the Catholic Church and by an Anglophone business elite in Montreal. In terms of divorce rates, family size, median income and access to secondary education, Quebec differed markedly from the English Canadian pattern. Since the end of the Second World War, Quebec society has modernised dramatically. Its essential demographic indices now converge towards the North American norm: low average family size, rising median income, high rates of access to secondary education, increasing secularisation and steadily declining influence on the part of the Catholic Church. This social revolution has been accompanied by a political and economic transformation which has seen French-speaking Quebeckers take over the levers of economic and political decision-making in their own society. They are now truly *maitres chez eux* – masters in their own house.

What is paradoxical is that exactly at the moment when Quebec has been losing, thanks to modernisation, much of what made it distinctive as a society, it has been insisting, ever more vehemently, on safeguarding the element of its distinctiveness which remains: language. Constitutionally, it is insisting on being recognised as a 'distinct society' in Canadian confederation at the precise historical moment when it is losing much of what made it truly distinctive. Finally, as it achieves its goals of self-determination, nationalist aspiration, instead of declining or abating, seems to be increasing, or at least showing no signs of abating.

Quebec seems to illustrate the paradox that as significant differences disappear between ethnic groups, they tend to focus, neuralgically, on the marginal elements of difference that remain; and that as they increase their margin of self-determination, they focus unhappily on the ever-decreasing margin which eludes their grasp.

As I have said, there is no necessary relation between the rise of nationalism and the increase of intolerance. Nevertheless, if what I have already said is true, the implications for the spread of intolerance are serious. We cannot assume that rising real incomes, modernisation, homogenisation, secularisation, the gradual levelling up of regions of backwardness, can be reliably counted on to reduce ethnic friction and intolerance. Indeed, although perhaps only as a transitional phenomenon, modernisation and 'progress' may exacerbate relations between ethnic groups and lead to an increase in intolerance. This should not be construed as an argument against taking economic disadvantage seriously: things might be worse in Northern Ireland had the British government not addressed both the sectional grievance of Catholics and the general economic disadvantage of the province. Likewise, in Quebec, the modernisation and secularisation of the province may be very good things in themselves, for those who benefit from them. My point is that they do not, by themselves, do anything to reconcile French-speaking Quebeckers to living beside English-speaking ones. Indeed, these processes may have the opposite result.

The analytical point to be made is that toleration is more dependent on values, culture and perception than it is on the facts of

difference. The reduction of 'objective' difference between competing groups does not necessarily, and by itself, lead to a reduction in
'subjective' suspicion. Indeed, as groups converge 'objectively', their
mutual intolerance may grow.

IV

Thus far, this discussion of the narcissism of minor difference has
focused on ethnic difference, especially on differences between
peoples who call themselves nations. But the same dynamic of
intolerance can be observed in the case of race. Skin colour is a
relatively minor difference; it certainly is no carrier of differences of
ability, talent or application. Economic differences within groups of
identical skin colour can be much more decisive in determining the
life chances of individuals than differences between racial groups.
Indeed, as the economic conditions of two groups of different race
converge towards each other one might expect their interests to
converge and their mutual identification to increase. The narcissism
of minor difference teaches us to expect a different result.

One could mention the example of wage-labouring whites in the
American South after the Civil War. As their economic condition
declined, their conditions of life began to converge with, though
they never actually approached, the poverty of most blacks. Marxist
and socialist labour organisers, from the 1930s through to the 1960s,
sought to persuade whites and blacks to recognise the convergence of
their economic and social interests. They sought, in other words, to
persuade them that their common 'class' interests transcended the
'racial' suspicions that divided them. These attempts did not succeed.
As economic conditions converged, suspicions among the 'red necks'
increased: it might even be the case that as the elements of personal
dignity and pride connected to economic performance were sum-
marily stripped away by the operations of the capitalist market,
dignity and pride came to repose exclusively in the one, unlosable
marker of identity which was skin colour.

The same paradoxical relation between economic and racial
markers of identity is observable among declining sections of the
white working class in Europe. It is precisely as economic pressures

force the convergence of white and black patterns of life and circumstance that white racial hostility becomes most explosive. Economic competition for jobs, and the divide-and-rule policies of employers, cannot explain this re-emphasis on skin colour as a marker of identity between groups. Whiteness is above all understood culturally and historically, as the badge of privilege and superiority, and hence as a marker of dignity and pride. In the imperial heyday these meanings went unchallenged; in a post-colonial, post-imperial world, the more these meanings are challenged the more they are insisted upon. Why should this be so?

It may be that among economically disadvantaged groups there are relatively fewer ways of achieving dignity, status and pride as individuals. Just as adherence to trade unions was once based on the simple, yet fundamentally sound intuition that economic advance could only be achieved collectively, not individually, so as class institutions of solidarity decay, and individual means of achievement remain blocked, the available sources of pride in neighbourhoods increasingly inhabited by 'foreign' people return to the collective element of skin colour. When white skin is then tattooed, as it often is, with national flags, skin colour and national symbols are bonded together into an identity which insists that nationality is or ought to be a function of race alone. Such flags can be seen on male, and sometimes on female, biceps from Wolverhampton to Leipzig in the Europe of the 1990s. It could be argued that they are to be seen wherever individuals cannot achieve individual success, wherever individuals are forced, by economic circumstances, into exclusively collective routes for the assertion of personal identity and pride. Racism, on this account, is the pride of those trapped in collective identities.

It would follow that racism might diminish if the trapped were freed, if the trapped had the means to pursue individual lives which would accord them measures and markers of achievement and pride. There must be some truth in this, though with the proviso already entered, that reduction of 'subjective' feelings of intolerance does not necessarily follow from reduction of 'objective' barriers between groups. Yet it might be true that toleration bears some relation to the possibility for individuation and individual achievement. A German

man who can show you his house, his car and a family as measures of his own pride rather than just his white skin may be less likely to wish to torch an immigrant hostel.

Yet the capacity to individuate yourself depends on much more than having a job and a home of one's own. It also means learning the capacity to think for oneself: that is, being able to cease absorbing collective identities without reflection; becoming self-conscious that one's personal identity may be different from the collective identity of colour. In this sense education is important, not simply as an avenue of mobility and individual achievement, but as a means of teaching self-reflexivity and critical thought, the tools for distancing the self from the collective identity.

All of this analysis runs counter to the proposition that intolerance is a consequence of modern competitive individualism and emerges in conditions of capitalist market anomie. On the contrary, it seems to me that the culture of individualism is the only reliable solvent of the hold of group identities and the racisms that go with them. To be sure, as I have already said, if the market fails, as it is failing upwards of twenty million unemployed young people in Europe alone, then it does create the conditions in which individuals must turn to group hatreds in order to assert and defend their identities. But, in principle, a culture which insists on individual responsibility, which links identity not to group ascription but to individual achievement, is much less likely to produce intolerance than one which continually reinscribes the individual in the group and which insists that the sources of the self's worth are all to be found in the collective.

The point here is somewhat paradoxical: the habits of mind necessary to toleration may have just as much to do with how persons view themselves and their relation to their own collective identities as they do with their attitudes towards others. The essential task in teaching 'toleration' is to help people see themselves as individuals, and then to see others as such; that is, to make problematic that unthought, unconsidered fusion of personal and group identity on which racism depends.

For racism and intolerance are, at a conceptual level, procedures of abstraction in which actual, real individuals in all their specificity are depersonalised and turned into ciphers or carriers of hated group characteristics. Often indeed such processes of abstraction have to struggle against the obdurate likeableness of the individual. Thus the notorious phrase, 'Some of my best friends are Jews but . . .', which recognises, in bitter joking form, the uncomfortable lack of consonance between actual real individual Jews one knows and the abstracted stereotypes one persists in believing in. When Othello is tormented by jealousy towards Desdemona – a jealousy at once sexual and racial – he finds himself struggling, in effect, with a process of abstraction in which the Desdemona he loves is successively reduced, by cancerous paranoia, from the particular woman he passionately loves to a white woman it is conventional for black men to hate. Only when such a reduction of her individuality is complete, when the object of his vengeance is an abstracted cipher, can he accomplish the vengeance which his paranoia desires.

Intolerance, as a sentiment of collective prejudice, has to struggle against, and eventually deny, more elementary patterns of human recognition and fellowship which function at the individual level. This would suggest that intolerance is a form of divided consciousness, in which abstract, conceptual, ideological hatred vanquishes concrete, real and individual moments of identification. This pattern of struggle is familiar enough and has a familiar ending: the Nazi camp commandant who falls in love with his Jewish maid, only to despatch her to the gas chambers; the white slave owner who maintains tender relations with individual slaves, only to insist the more vehemently that slaves are not persons but property; the British racialist who has individual relations with Pakistani restaurant owners or shopkeepers but who believes, nonetheless, that Pakistanis in general should be sent 'home'.

What appears to be happening in these familiar, even clichéd instances, is that a moment of intra-human recognition, which abolishes the difference between them, is violently denied by the stronger party and an abstracted, 'ideological' difference is reinstated in order to maintain the dignity and power of the oppressor. For, from the oppressor's point of view, the moment of human recognition decisively threatens both his identity and power: a camp commandant who begins to spare his Jewish lovers will not be a camp commandant very long; a slave owner who decides slaves are persons may not be able to retain his estate very long; a racialist who admits he rather likes Pakistanis and values the services they provide might have to consider the possibility that whiteness of skin does not confer the right to decide who deserves to belong in Britain and who does not. In this sense, therefore, an 'individualised' encounter between oppressor and oppressed, ruler and ruled, racialist and victim, is so fraught with possibilities of loss that one side at least has a standing interest in keeping relations enclosed within the abstraction of collective prejudice. For the abstracted, collective plane of intolerance keeps power relations as they are: it is intended to prevent those moments of human recognition which make intolerance ashamed.

Against such collective abstraction, the oppressed, as I have been calling the victims of intolerance, have always made a double appeal: to their individuality, and to their humanity. The two claims are distinct. In situations of extremity, a victim who recognises an individual among the group of his oppressors will desperately seek to evoke their former relations in the hope that the particular oppressor may exempt him from the general fate and make an exception in his case. Failing that, the victim will appeal, not to his individuality, but to the common human identity he shares with the oppressor. 'Hath a Jew not eyes?' is the general form of such appeals.

Since it is, needless to say, more than evident that a Jew hath eyes, the question is why intolerant beliefs which deny this evidence should retain such plausibility. Why is it that the victim's twin appeal – to individuality and to common humanity – so often falls on deaf ears? The narcissism of minor difference does help us to explain why this failure of human recognition so perennially occurs.

Modern liberal societies operate their systems of distributive justice. They value, reward, promote or punish individual difference and juridically, at least, ignore collective differences. The law is nominally blind to differences of race, colour, creed, ethnicity, gender and sexual orientation; and highly discriminatory in relation to individual difference at the level of action and intention. Likewise, our systems of reward and promotion spend endless amounts of ingenuity sifting minute differences in individual ability, and attempt studiously to deny the salience of collective difference; or if they take collective difference into account – as in systems of positive discrimination – do so, not in order to advantage collectivities, but in order to level the playing field of competition for previously disadvantaged individuals.

The utopia at which such liberal societies aim is a fully tolerant world. While it is obvious that such a world would be desirable, the question is whether it is psychologically plausible. For a moment, let us imagine what such a world might look like. It would not be a world which had banished anger, hatred, suspicion or dislike. It would merely be a world in which all angers, hatreds, suspicions or dislikes would be purely private or between individuals. That is to say, if one disliked people it would be entirely because of their characteristics as individuals: their moral or aesthetic characteristics or their opinions. You would not dislike them because they were black or white, rich or poor, female or male, homosexual or heterosexual, German or Chinese, but simply because they were, as individuals, boring, untrustworthy, vain, stupid or whatever. In such a liberal utopia, in other words, interpersonal aggression would have an outlet, but it would be directed at real, as opposed to aggregated, abstracted collective entities called races, classes, genders and so on. This utopia helps us to make clear at least that a tolerant world is not necessarily a world free of invidious comparison, still less a world free of hatred and aggression. It is merely a place in which individuals are not disadvantaged by virtue of adventitious collective identities like race, colour, creed, gender or sexual orientation. The question is whether such a world is psychologically plausible. Is a world of pure individuals possible? Or do all individuals need collective identities, and because they need them, must they construct invidious collective comparisons upon them? In other words, is some element of collective intolerance the inevitable price we have to pay for having the collective boundaries necessary to human identity itself? This question arises because the liberal goal of a tolerant society is constantly accused of psychological implausibility, of demanding of Old Adam and Eve a redemption beyond their powers.

The question is not whether individuals need collective identities: history shows they self-evidently do. The issue is whether they need to use collective identities to make invidious comparisons; whether such negative comparisons are essential to identity formation itself. A potential contradiction thus opens up between liberal individualism as utopia, and to some degree as a juridical practice, and psychic reality. Freud's theory about the narcissism of minor difference, however, does suggest that while some measure of collective antagonism is inevitable in human relations, this antagonism is not fixed or immutable. It changes its objects. In the British class system, for example, groups who once loathed each other because of the vast gulf between their economic fortunes now merely make fun of each other because they dress or speak differently. In South Africa, racial groups who once believed they inhabited distinct, unvisitable moral and cultural universes, are at least engaged in intense ethnic competition within a democratic framework. Their perceptions of each other have been transformed in the last generation: their narcissism continues to fix on difference but with fewer murderous and inhuman consequences. Freud suggests that hostility and antagonism are built into the human negotiation of difference. That is the pessimistic message. The hopeful message, and the one I conclude with, is that these differences can become less murderous with time. To the degree that individuals can ever learn to think for themselves, become true individuals, they can free themselves, one by one, from the deadly dynamic of the narcissism of minor difference.

Notes

1. S. Freud, 'The Taboo of Virginity', in *On Sexuality*, Pelican Freud Library, Vol. VII, Harmondsworth, Penguin, 1977, pp. 271–2.
2. S. Freud, 'Group Psychology and the Analysis of the Ego', in *Civilisation, Society and Religion*, Pelican Freud Library, vol. XII, Harmondsworth, Penguin, 1985, pp. 130–1.
3. S. Freud, 'Civilization and its Discontents', in *Civilisation Society and Religion*, Pelican Freud Library, vol. XII, Harmondsworth, Penguin, 1985, p. 304.
4. John Locke, *A Letter Concerning Toleration,* Buffalo, N. Y., Prometheus Books, 1990, p. 21.
5. Michael Ignatieff, *Blood and Belonging*, London, Vintage, 1994.
6. Ernest Gellner, *Nations and Nationalism*, Oxford, Blackwell, 1983.

Chapter 7

The politics of intolerance
Helena Kennedy

Democracy is the most valued and also perhaps the vaguest of political concepts in the modern world. As we know too well, very diverse political systems describe themselves as democracies, but essentially, in a democracy, political power is in the hands of the whole adult population, and no smaller group has the right to rule. However, and as John Stuart Mill remarked in his essay *On Liberty*, democracy can be tyranny by the majority.[1] Liberal values such as freedom of expression and the freedom to exercise a lifestyle of one's own, however unconventional, as long as it hurts no one, can be seriously at risk in a majoritarian democracy. In Mill's view, ill-informed people are prone to intolerance of opinion and behaviour and are likely to persecute people who do not fit in. We can list all too many examples which prove the correctness of this theory.

Tolerance and human rights are therefore essential to democracy. Without tolerance, the foundations for democracy cannot be strengthened and respect for human rights cannot be maintained. And without all three – tolerance, human rights and democracy – there cannot be peace.

The cultural shift

In 1983 Lord Scarman, in his Morrell Memorial Address, described the English tradition of tolerance – live and let live – as one of the tenets upon which the common law was built.[2] He had just chaired the Scarman Inquiry into the race disturbances in Brixton and was very mindful of the discrimination experienced by minorities. Always a man ahead of his time, he argued in his Address for a Bill of Rights, believing that a backdrop of principle would inform the courts and create legal coherence. All in all he was optimistic that liberty was so cherished by the British people that as long as we were vigilant our liberties were safe. I am not sure he would be so sanguine today, for the last decade has seen individualism, consumption and blatant self-interest promoted into acceptable modes of behaviour. In this thrusting new world, the populace is divided into winners and losers, employed and un-employed, successful and unsuccessful. The measure of worth is that of 'value added' and 'cost effectiveness', and the ugly language of the marketplace. The nation has been seduced by the notion that a deregulation which allowed entrepreneurs to run free in the money markets would make us all the beneficiary of trickle-down economics. Instead, the divisions between rich and poor have become more marked. We have not seen everyone embraced by the benefits of such policies; rather we have seen increasing exclusion, which now poses a serious threat to social cohesion. Aspects of British life, of which we rightly felt proud, are being undermined. There has been a denigration of public service so that those who choose to work in the fields of education, health care, social work, legal aid, the police, the probation or prison service are all seen to be losers, lacking the entrepreneurial drive that is idealised in the present climate. Under-valuing of those crucial functions – the care of the sick or needy, the teaching of our young, the maintenance of the social fabric – engenders low morale, with the inevitable consequence that those activities become unworthy and, therefore, ineffective. In abandoning our *economic* destiny to the marketplace we seem to be abandoning our *moral* destiny to it as well.

We have also seen anti-discriminatory initiatives derided as poli-tically correct, and equality of opportunity insidiously pushed off the agenda as an issue of national concern. Lip service is paid to equal opportunities for all, but we seem to be shutting our eyes to the damage that injustice and discrimination are doing, as well as to the frustration, bitterness and hopelessness that they create in people. Tolerance is now being presented by some public and media figures as a good thing only in small doses. Yet all our historic experience tells us that a just and peaceful society is only possible where there is tolerance and respect for diversity.

It is fashionable now to decry the sixties as the decade when moral decay set in, when 'doing your own thing' was the motto of the day. Yet for commitment to unrepentant individualism the eighties has perhaps greater claim to social destructiveness. This characterisation of decadent sixties liberalism takes no account of the concern with moral imperatives such as war and peace, racial and sex discrimination, poverty and corruption – moral imperatives with which a generation became passionately engaged. There was no shame then in having a social conscience, no dismissal of commitment to such issues as a manifestation of 'wetness' or the display of a bleeding heart. The sixties was the decade in which it was recognised that our society was no longer homogeneous and that anti-discrimination legislation was necessary in pursuit of equality and justice. Imposing one's views upon the unwilling was deprecated and the need for tolerance was identified as crucial to the well-being of the community.

Members of an organised society need to share common goals and aspirations, what Lord Devlin, our great jurist, called 'the invisible bond', which holds society together. Once tolerance is surrendered, one of society's crucial welding mechanisms is weakened too. Are we living in a nation 'at ease with itself', to quote John Major? Do the vitriolic attacks by government ministers upon single mothers, New Age travellers, ravers, gypsies, immigrants, refugees, scrounging unemployed, feckless youth and inferior Europeans encourage peaceful co-existence? These messages do not inculcate a tolerance of diversity, but breed a culture of adversity and alienation.

Tolerance is particularly invoked in relation to race, religion, sexuality and freedom of speech, and I shall reflect upon some of those issues in turn, but the growing marginalisation of certain sections of our communities because they do not conform to the dominant aspirations cannot be ignored. Not only is the marginalisation another manifestation of intolerance, but marginalised groups themselves are likely to feed upon their own hostilities and foster their own forms of intolerance. New provisions under the Criminal Justice and Public Order Act to control travellers, ravers, squatters and anti-hunt demonstrators have considerable implications for the right of assembly and protest. But these provisions also stoke the fires of social antagonism and ostracism, which are enormously destructive.

Ethnicity and conflict

Ethnic diversity is a feature of all societies, but how such diversity is perceived, and the importance attached to it, vary greatly between regions and over time. The same ethnic markers – physical differences, cultural practices, or religious beliefs – may be completely ignored in one society, while they are considered extremely significant in another. Ethnicity, however, is only one of the ways in which people identify themselves: others being family, community, nationality, class, gender, age and other group characteristics considered important to people's sense of self-identity. Ethnicity under certain circumstances has a propensity to become 'totalising', displacing other loyalties and obligations to become the sole basis of identity. Then the likelihood of racial conflict increases, because people's identities and alliances take on a single rather than a multiple focus, leading to a polarisation of social divisions.

The answer offered by many people is to ignore difference, and insist upon assimilation. 'Every society should become like us!' is the rallying cry of the right-wing ideologues who have decried multicultural education and social programmes. Yet, paradoxically, it is preservation rather than assimilation that is vital in order for ethnic identity to develop the flexibility and tolerance necessary to move beyond its destructive polarising forms. For it is precisely when ethnic or cultural identity is threatened that it becomes important to people. When they do not feel free to express their ethnicity, through speaking their own language, practising their own cultural traditions and transmitting them to their children, they are less likely to develop a sense of civic identity or a feeling that they share common goals with the larger society.

Moreover, a sense of civic identity cannot be forced on people. They must adopt it voluntarily, and this will happen only when they feel that their society respects them and responds to their common needs, including their need for a sense of ethnic identity. That is why it is so important for a government and its ministers to foster an appreciation of diversity in all its forms. Rather than using the language of exclusion, they should be creating the conditions that allow all groups within society to feel a sense of common purpose and mutual respect. Similarly, policies which enlarge the gap between rich and poor intensify insecurity and are likely to exacerbate ethnic tensions and provide fertile ground for racism and the blaming of immigrants for social problems. It is not coincidental that we are seeing increased racial attacks and harassment of ethnic minority communities. Likewise, strategies that enhance inequality, especially if class divisions coincide with ethnic divisions, will inevitably strengthen perceptions of discrimination and victimisation by marginalised ethnic groups. It is not only perceptions, of course, as the incidence of black unemployment is disproportionately high and reflects serious discriminatory practices in recruitment. The absence of legal aid for industrial tribunals means such practices are rarely challenged.

Religion and social cohesion

It is, therefore, essential to provide the conditions which will encourage all groups within a society to feel a shared interest in the society as a whole. The creation of a sense of civic identity and inclusion can be achieved in many different ways. For example, I myself believe that it is not fostered by having an established church, and it is interesting that our king-in-waiting, when interviewed by Jonathan Dimbleby, displayed an unease at the role of king as Defender of the Faith, indicating that he saw the role of monarch more as defender of *faith*, and referring specifically to the need to include Catholics, Jews and Muslims.

I also believe that the blasphemy laws are not only an inhibition to freedom of speech but an anachronism in a society which is multicultural. The statute protects only the established church, and when Muslim elders made application to invoke the legislation against Salman Rushdie's *The Satanic Verses*, the courts refused to interpret the law as extending to other religions. While liberals celebrated what they perceived as the triumph of free speech, it was clear that a hierarchy of interests still operates in a divisive way.

It is also interesting that it is not an offence to dismiss people in England on the grounds of their religion. Employers have an unfettered right on this ground even though it is specifically prohibited in Northern Ireland. Here, then, in the discriminatory legislation which governs religion, we find one manifestation of intolerance.

Political sanctuary

The attack upon asylum seekers is yet another manifestation of growing intolerance. Like the sacred right of silence, an ancient protection within our criminal law, the rights of refugees are now being sacrificed to a vulgar populism. Moreover, the new policy of exclusion at our borders seems to be directed at people of colour and the message received by our resident immigrant community is that they are here on sufferance because we will not let in any more like them. This, surely, cannot be a way of creating a nation at ease with itself, nor yet a way of strengthening the ties that bind us.

The proposals for legislation governing asylum seekers will effectively create a white list of countries which will be deemed to be safe, and the assumption therefore is that they are unlikely to produce real refugees.[3] What the public are not being told by government is that we grant asylum to very few applicants as it is under the current law. For example, the Home Office figures show that in 1994 we admitted 5,000 asylum seekers, of whom only 1,100 were finally granted asylum.

Additionally, the publication of a Home Office report which conflicted with government policy on asylum was delayed. This report was based on a study of 263 asylum seekers and concluded that the majority came to Britain with substantial work and educational qualifications. This, of course, contradicted the pronouncements made by government ministers that asylum seekers are really poor economic immigrants who will become financial burdens on the taxpayer.

Here, then, is another area in which intolerance is increasing rather than diminishing.

Sexuality

Sexuality provides yet another example. The family values campaigns by government have in some areas backfired upon them, particularly when 'back to basics' seems to a number of senior political figures to mean 'back to my place'. The sexual scandals of political figures are only important in that they expose hypocrisy and double standards. However, the family as cornerstone of society has also been used to attack unconventional families, single mothers and particularly homosexuals.

Thus, the introduction of Clause 28 prevents local authorities from spending public money on promoting or assisting homosexuality. As a result advice centres and other support resources cannot be public-funded. Local authorities cannot spend money or hold meetings or publish leaflets for their employees in an attempt to end victimisation of and prejudice towards homosexual members of staff. Not only does this amount to an obvious and flagrant abuse of human rights but it also prevents those homosexuals who pay local taxes from receiving the kinds of community benefit they should expect.

The age of consent for homosexuals and heterosexuals also remains different (eighteen and sixteen respectively). The British government stands alone with Portugal amongst European countries in refusing to allow homosexuality in the armed forces. Dismissal from employment or a refusal to employ on the grounds of homosexuality is not unlawful.

A bill of rights

These are just some of the areas in which Britain is an increasingly intolerant society, and the European Court of Human Rights has found against the United Kingdom in all these areas – and more. In his book *A Bill of Rights for Britain*, Professor Ronald Dworkin notes, as I do, that the culture of liberty is declining. He writes:

> Great Britain was once a fortress for freedom. It claimed the great philosophers of liberty – Milton and Locke and Paine and Mill. Its legal tradition is irradiated with liberal ideas; that people accused of

crime are presumed to be innocent, that no one owns another's conscience, that a man's home is his castle. But now Britain offers less formal legal protection to central freedoms than most of its neighbours in Europe.[4]

Like Dworkin, and like an increasing number of people in Britain today, I too believe that in the interests of liberty we must incorporate the European Convention of Human Rights into our domestic law. However, I also believe we should thereafter engage in a period of national consultation as a process towards the creation of our own tailor-made charter of rights. Until people have a sense of themselves as citizens with rights and obligations to each other and to their community, we will see fragmentation within our society.

The current picture may look bleak but I am increasingly convinced that just as the notion of democratic rights – the right of each person to participate in the democratic process – was the driving idea of the nineteenth and early twentieth centuries, so the notion of substantive rights will be seen in retrospect as the dominant idea of the last decades of the twentieth century. As surely as the idea of democratic rights dramatically changed the lives of so many, so the idea of human rights will be seen, looking back, to have improved immeasurably the lot of the disadvantaged in our society, and indeed throughout the world.

Understandably, there are sceptics who doubt that the law has any real role to play in reversing discrimination or redressing systematic inequities. And while I accept that fundamental change is secured politically, it is important that we also recognise the law's role in regulating our social relations. In fulfilling that function it sends out powerful messages which resonate throughout society. As far back as the seventeenth century John Locke wrote in his *Letter Concerning Toleration*: 'If men could live peaceably and quietly together . . . there would be no need of magistrates or politics, which were only made to preserve men in this world from the fraud and violence of one another.'[5]

Rights are a necessary part of our social relations and they have to be guaranteed. They are, of course, not a recent invention. The strange British claim is that our rights live within the silence of the law. This has meant that British lawyers have been responsive rather than creative, which in turn has meant that when we were inspired to follow the course of other jurisdictions and adopted legislation directed at rights such as equal opportunities and race relations legislation, we had no intellectual tradition to make it work. We travelled down the Aristotelian road that defined equality as treating like with like. Even the Enlightenment, which provided us with the basis for our contemporary notion of rights, failed adequately to acknowledge that rights are meaningless if we are blind to the real forces that give one power while relegating another to impotence, that accord wealth to one group while condemning others to poverty. Our legal system has rarely been insightful about such disparity, and for most of its history the common law unapologetically distinguished between people according to their religion, sex, race and family status.

However, what we are seeing develop in the international legal community is a new notion of rights, and a different concept of equality. It is a concept of equality based on the idea that it is generally wrong and unacceptable to discriminate against people on the basis of personal characteristics such as race or sex. As such, we have seen a shift to ameliorative or substantive equality, and a recognition that treating as equal those who are unequal only creates further inequality. The new concept of equality looks at the reality of people's lives and asks what discrimination really does to them. It does not accept that the law is necessarily neutral and it challenges formal justice.

Nonetheless, these concepts have been slow to enter our legal thinking in Britain and will in my view only flower when rooted in principle in a Bill of Rights. The first time that rights were given legal force was in the ten amendments to the United States Constitution. With these, the founding fathers invented a new purpose of government – to protect individual rights from community consensus. This suggests a very different concept of rights from that which developed in Europe. Americans today still refer to the concept of natural rights, whereas within Europe we draw upon the traditions of an international human rights movement established after the Second World War and the hideous experiences of the Holocaust. But there may be lessons we can learn from the American model.

Ira Glasser, of the American Civil Liberties Union, argues that four principles underlie the doctrine of natural rights – diversity, personal sovereignty, equality and the duty to resist oppression.[6] The ACLU is keen to defend this doctrine because it connects the organisation historically to the founding of the American state. Of course, the doctrine implies that certain rights pre-exist human society; that rights are there to be discovered and are not the product of a particular society and time. The idea of natural rights also entails considerable hostility to state power – and resistance to the general encroachment of state power is a vital part of American culture. For a variety of reasons, it is harder to invoke this doctrine outside the US, and in consequence any British Bill of Rights should more appropriately be based on international human rights documents and should respect the democratic role in resolving conflicts of rights. In this respect, the experience of both Canada and New Zealand may be more appropriate to the British experience.

Canada introduced a Charter of Rights and Freedoms in 1982, and a review of the case law is instructive. What is most interesting is the quality of the legal argument and the assistance available to the judiciary to inform their judgements through *amicus* briefs. Thus, the Charter makes it possible for interest groups to present arguments in cases of public importance so that, for example, cases before the Supreme Court on an issue of women's reproductive freedom will entitle the National Association of Women's Organisations to put their case before the court.

More generally, in Canada human rights codes and the Charter of Rights have played and continue to play an important role in fostering substantive equality and preventing discrimination, and their effect extends beyond individual cases decided. They have encouraged a wider and more general climate of tolerance in which millions of Canadians who have never appeared before a human rights tribunal now accept the immorality, in employment for example, of discriminating on the basis of personal characteristics which have nothing to do with whether someone can do the job or not. Of course, it would be a delusion to see a charter of rights as a panacea for Britain's ills, but it would certainly be a bolt of electricity into the body politic as well as the body legal. It could also be a very important educative tool. It could be used to generate understanding and a climate of tolerance if enough collective energy went into its creation

It seems to me that the philosopher and political theorist John Rawls has devised a very good mechanism for the creation of the rules of a tolerant society.[7] He calls it 'the veil of ignorance'. This calls on us to ignore certain basic social facts about ourselves. Thus, we are to imagine a person who is ignorant of his or her sex, age, class or race. What social institutions would such a person think to be fair? The point is that if you do not know whether you are to be a slave or a ruler, a man or a woman, black or white, able-bodied or disabled, heterosexual or homo-sexual, Protestant or Jew, you will not opt for unfair rules because you could end up on the wrong side of the bargain. It will be well worth remembering Rawls's device when we come to create the perfect Bill of Rights.

Tolerance has a pivotal role in helping to define and realise so many freedoms within our society. It is essential to freedom of belief, racial and gender equity, fundamental human rights, and justice for all irrespective of difference. It is crucial to the creation of a more enlightened and cohesive society. Tolerance only persists where there is social justice. Let me conclude with the poem of Juan Gonzales Rose from his *Carta a Maria Therese*:

> I ask myself now
> Why I do not limit my love
> to the sudden roses
> the tides or June
> the moons over the sea?
> Why have I had to love
> the rose and justice
> the sea and justice
> justice and the light?

Those of us who are privileged, who are 'included' rather than 'excluded', have a duty to speak out. We must reclaim and restate the values of tolerance and justice.

Notes

1. John Stuart Mill, *On Liberty*, Harmondsworth, Penguin, 1978. First published 1879.
2. Lord Scarman, 'Toleration and the Law', in S. Mendus and D. Edwards (eds), *On Toleration,* Oxford, Oxford University Press, 1987, pp. 49–62.
3. The Asylum and Immigration Bill, 1995–6, which became the Asylum and Immigration Act, 1996.
4. Ronald Dworkin, *A Bill of Rights for Britain,* London, Chatto and Windus, 1990.
5. John Locke, *A Letter on Toleration,* in J. Horton and S. Mendus (eds), *John Locke: A Letter Concerning Toleration in Focus*, London, Routledge, 1991.
6. Ira Glasser, *Visions of Liberty: The Bill of Rights for All Americans*, New York, Arcade, 1991.
7. John Rawls, *A Theory of Justice*, Oxford, Oxford University Press, 1971.

Chapter 8

Religious toleration in the UK: is it feasible?
Julia Neuberger

The UK, Britain in particular rather than Northern Ireland, prides itself on its tolerance. In part, Britain describes itself as tolerant because of its relatively free admission of minorities who were fleeing persecution in other countries up to 1905, and because of its tolerant messages thereafter. Some of those so-called 'tolerant' messages could be challenged, in that it is the case that the 1905 Aliens' Act was passed in the space of a single week to keep out the hordes of Jews pressing into Britain from Russia and Poland – the so-called Pale of Settlement – after appalling massacres of Jews in the Kishinev pogroms and others. It is also true that Britain's behaviour over East African Asians in 1968 shows little in the way of toleration. It was one of the most disgraceful episodes in modern British history, when a Labour government (this does not divide along party lines) ruled retroactively against the entry of the East African Asians who were British citizens. It was not until the case went to the European Commission on Human Rights that they came, slowly, by a voucher system.

In 1995, I served on the Glidewell Panel, which was set up by a number of charities, to examine the likely effects of the changes in asylum legislation, and particularly the effects of removing benefit from asylum seekers whilst they waited for their appeals to be heard. We looked at the effect that living on the street might have on their family life, and we particularly looked at the effect on children, who might have to be taken into care as a result of local authorities having a duty of care for the children but not the adults. The main conclusion drawn by the Glidewell Panel was that it was legitimate and proper to have a system of appeals, and that such a system should be fair and seen to be fair. If there were terrible delays in the system, that was the fault of government and not of the asylum seekers. They should not be penalised for the slow system which necessitated them waiting, often several years, to appeal.

I still feel that that is correct, and have been much delighted by the decisions that have come from our courts declaring local authorities to have a duty to provide basic help to asylum seekers. I was particularly impressed by Mr Justice Collins arguing on 8 October 1996 that the government cannot have intended to leave asylum seekers who were lawfully in Britain to starve or become destitute on the streets, at the risk of grave illness or even death. He noted that 'the prospect of asylum seekers being taken to hospital, nursed back to health, discharged on to the streets, allowed to fall ill again and so on is hardly attractive, yet that would be the effect of the constructions favoured by the respondents' (the three London boroughs who were answering the case of the asylum seekers). He then continued: 'The right to life is a fundamental human right. It is one which the law will protect . . . it has to be assumed that Parliament has legislated in accord with it.' In other words, Parliament, according to his ruling, cannot have intended asylum seekers to starve. And local authorities will have to provide for the asylum seekers if they are 'satisfied that any of them have no other means of support and therefore are in need of care and attention, since such a need may exist where a person is unable to provide for himself'. He then added that if Parliament had intended asylum seekers to be assisted in no way at all, other than in hospital care, 'it would almost certainly put itself in breach of the European Convention on Human Rights and of the Geneva Convention'. Presumably, he was arguing so strongly in his judgement because he felt that acting in dereliction of the duty to give basic assistance was a denial of a fundamental human right. And this comes surely from a concept of what the nature of a civilised society is: that it is one in which we help those who cannot help themselves, and amongst genuine asylum seekers are many who have had the most appalling treatment at the hands of governments, including the experience of torture. Mr Justice Collins's comments surely embody, even if in somewhat minimalist way, what might be understood as toleration on the part of the state.

Asylum seekers coming to official interview may not be able to report details of their persecution and torture experiences, because of the mental dissociation from the experience, enhanced by the pressure of the asylum experience. This can be more difficult the more they have been persecuted, and it can therefore be very difficult for some people to declare themselves as asylum seekers as soon as they arrive in Britain – which is what they are now required to do. Indeed, the lack of understanding about the nature of the experience of having been tortured was one of the things that was so depressing about the whole parliamentary debate on this subject. Toleration was not a key feature. It was therefore a real pleasure to hear the Duke of Norfolk, not usually known as one of the country's great radicals, speaking firmly and forcefully about torture, and how he had seen it and understood it, and how you could not necessarily see the scars. The Medical Foundation for the Victims of Torture and post-traumatic stress specialists all argue firmly that it is only after a relationship of trust has grown up between a torture survivor and his or her lawyer, doctor or other helper that one begins to get the complete story. So how can one expect to get the story of torture, get people to say that they are asylum seekers after torture, at the point of entry? How can the state require it? It is not reasonable to expect people whose experience of officialdom is so appalling to be able to speak in a foreign language to someone they do not know at the point of entry after a frightening and often difficult journey. But that is what we now require, to our everlasting shame.

It is worth asking why we require this. First, there is racism in the attitude to asylum seekers, although no one will admit that. The majority of asylum seekers in Britain are black or brown, and, unlike other immigrants, they are real outsiders, begging to come here, not coming as some kind of right. How we treat people from minority ethnic communities is always a test of how civilised a society we are. I know of no better commentator on that issue than Dipak Nandy, first director of the Runnymede Trust, who wrote: 'It is the duty of politicians to heed public opinion. It is equally the duty of politicians to educate public opinion. But nothing in the theory of democratic politics requires politicians to give way to popular prejudices especially where the rights of minorities are at stake.'[1]

Similarly, A. J. Sherman describes prevailing attitudes most poignantly in his book on the response of Britain to the refugees from the Third Reich between 1933 and 1945, a book in which he interestingly castigates the Anglo-Jewish community for its lack of activity less than other commentators have done:

> the refugee crisis brought painfully into consciousness the ambiguities of assimilation, especially in a country as relatively insular and monochromatic as Great Britain in the pre-war period; and their anxiety over the numbers and conspicuousness of the refugees, their sheer foreignness, the likelihood that they would stir not only anti-Semitism but anti-German feeling still latent from the First World War, was shared by government officials as well as Jewish communal leaders.[2]

The Anglo-Jewish community was inclined to keep its head down and to show almost obsequious gratitude when non-Jews showed concern, offered help, or expressed their shared outrage at events in Nazi Germany.

That fear of being noticed, particularly after the war started, led to very little campaigning for fellow Jews in Europe. There was a war on. British Jews must be seen to be Britishly involved in the war effort, and not to get diverted by uniquely Jewish concerns. Yet, at the same time, the records of the Central British Fund suggest a huge effort on behalf of those trapped in Nazi Germany as the war started, and considerable campaigning, and pressure on the Home Office, to let more people in, which may, at the time, have seemed all that one could do. Indeed, the estimates of the numbers of refugees allowed in, as given to Parliament, seem to have been consistently undercounted, as the total number was probably around seventy thousand, whilst the Home Secretary reported 49,500 in October 1939. Perhaps the officials knew when to keep quiet about what was going on, and even more importantly, perhaps they were more kindly disposed than later critics have suggested that they were. Toleration on the part of the state is possible, as the under-reporting of numbers of German Jewish refugees makes clear. And yet we had the East African Asians case, and we now have the Asylum Act, which is cruel in its treatment of those who are genuine asylum seekers, people who have suffered torture, hardship, persecution, and horrors of other nameless breeds. We show them little toleration. Instead, they must make themselves understood to us, before they have the chance to learn anything.

So can we be tolerant in this society? And, if so, can we be tolerant beyond the normal racial and ethnic boundaries, and in a more genuinely religious way? Can we look to the Church of England, the established church, and some of its recent magnificent statements about Jews and Muslims, and regard it as a protector of other faiths beyond Anglican Christianity? Will Prince Charles, when he is king, really be a 'defender of faith', or will he remain, as his forebears before him, Defender of *the* Faith, the Protestant Christian faith in its rare form of Anglicanism as practised by the Church of England?

In my lifetime, I believe we have become less tolerant. I believe we had a better chance of being genuinely religiously tolerant as a society in the days of multicultural education (now much sneered at) than we do now. I felt that particularly strongly after spending six months in the USA on a Harkness Fellowship. Religion is a private matter in the US, unlike our country with, in England anyway, its established church. In Britain, acts of worship take place daily, or at least regularly, in our schools, and, after the 1988 Education Act, are now supposed to be broadly Christian. In the US, you might see an act of allegiance to the American flag, but you would not find an act of worship in a state-supported school.

The historical reasons for that are well-known. The foundation of the early states as havens from religious persecution led to a firm decision to keep church and state separate. Religious influences have nevertheless bitten deep into the life of the country, and even though America is one of the most deeply evangelised countries in the Western world, with estimates of regular church attendance ranging from 50 per cent to 80 per cent of the population, compared with our pathetic 10 per cent or so and 2–3 per cent in cities, within education, within the public provision of goods and services, religion and the state are unconnected.

The politico-historical reasons, then, are well known. But there are other reasons, just as well known but far less frequently added into the equation. Amongst these are the pride which the US takes in being a country of immigrants. When the Ellis Island and Statue of Liberty Committee were trying to raise the money for the museum of immigration at Ellis Island, they could count on the pride of most Americans in being of immigrant stock, and know that they would wish to help perpetuate the memory of how they came for future generations. They hit on a brilliant marketing ploy. Everyone who sent $100 or more for the museum had his or her name engraved into the wall surrounding the museum grounds. The money flowed unceasingly. But if we tried, those of us of immigrant stock such as I am, to do the same here there are countless people who are also of immigrant stock who would wish to deny it. There are far, far more, for related reasons, who would not really know that they had foreign blood in them at all. Yet the number of people in England who can genuinely say that they can trace their ancestry back to the Norman conquest – an immigration of sorts, if you like – or the Saxon period, of which the same can be said, is precious small. Britain is also a land of immigrants, though less positively so, and less recently so. But we are a nation made up of Saxons and Normans, Vikings, Danes and Jutes, Huguenots and Dutch traders, Lombards and Germans, Jews and Irish, Chinese, African, West Indians, Pakistanis, Bangladeshis, Indians, and more. Moreover, we have always been an island open to invasion and immigration, and that has significantly altered the population profile.

I am labouring this point because it is essential to realise that we are no less of a country of immigration, historically speaking, than the US (though in recent decades we have been), even though our attitude to immigration has been entirely different. Where diversity has been celebrated in the US, it has been discouraged in the UK. Where everyone wore a dual identity with pride in the US (African-American, Irish-American, Italian-American, Jewish-American) the British, whatever their own origins, have always felt happier with the idea that we would approach a cultural unity, that diversity was a sign of weakness, and education was the key to making children of immigrant parents, with the connivance and encouragement of those parents in many cases, into true little Brits.

That was never very satisfactory, and in my community it led to a tendency for Jews involved in wider public life to lose some of their Jewish involvement. The two could not easily go hand in hand, in the minds of those newly educated little Brits, and possibly in the eyes of the wider population. This does not suggest that someone who is interested in political and cultural life on the wider British stage cannot be involved in Jewish life. That is patently untrue. But it does suggest that that has, on the whole, to take a back seat if life on the wider stage is to be pursued actively – and that therefore the Jewish scene is duller, less intellectual, less genuinely political, than it might otherwise be. In the US, where being a practising Jew is commonplace, Jews play their full part on the American cultural and political stage, and have a satisfying religious and cultural life, running successfully in tandem.

Now, I am not suggesting for one moment that the US has got it right. In terms of deprivation, access to goods and services, particularly in the fields of housing, health and education, African-Americans and Hispanics are appallingly badly served. Nor have I ever seen such ghettoisation of the inner city and heard, so frequently, the thinking on the part of academics and liberals, even the politically correct, that the only thing to do is to go and live in the suburbs, leaving the downtown areas to the African-Americans and the Hispanics. At the same time, however, there is a pride, an acceptance of cultural diversity, an acceptance of religious diversity, which is very refreshing.

One reason for that is the strict division between church and state. Pressure is building up in the US, largely as a result of dissatisfaction with the public schools in many inner-city areas, to fund the church schools, which would be totally contrary to the present provisions, and arguably unconstitutional. But that pressure is significant. And we see it in reverse in the UK, just because we do have an established church, and all that goes with it. Once we argue, as we essentially have, that education in our state schools is to be in some respect or other broadly Christian, we are saying that those who cannot describe any part of their identity, neither their present nor their past, as 'broadly Christian' do not fit. The escape route from a straight accusation of religious intolerance has always been the voluntary aided sector. Because there are Church of England schools, run by the church, and funded largely by the state, it is clear that there must be Catholic schools, at least if we do not wish to have an outright rebellion on our hands. And the growth of Catholic schools rested at least in part on the relationship with Ireland and the Irish. Then, when Jewish immigration became a serious issue, or should I say problem, in the 1880s, running on to the early years of this century, there were questions about Jewish schools, because Jews have been here for so long, and all those dietary requirements and so on. We must have Catholic schools, obviously we have C of E schools. But Muslim schools?

We have, as yet, no voluntary aided Muslim schools.[3] This is not for want of trying on the part of the Muslim population. The numbers of Muslims in the UK is something around one million people, with a rising birthrate, and clear patterns of settlement that would make Muslim schools, if they were felt to be desirable, easy to fill and easy to run. There are some 350,000 Jews in the UK, but there are voluntary aided Jewish schools, and one in six Jewish children go to them. What is the problem?

Let me try and spell out the problem. First, let me say that I myself wish we did not have religious-run schools. I would far rather that we educated children of all religions and ethnic origins together. But given that we have sectarian education at all, given that government took years to fund *non*-sectarian schools in Northern Ireland, given that we have an established church, it is strange to me that we have no voluntary aided Muslim schools.

One argument often adduced in the polite dining rooms of the chattering classes is that Muslims are a relatively new population in the UK. It is true that the significant Muslim population dates back to the fifties and early sixties. But that is thirty years ago or more. The same liberals in the chattering classes argue hard that women, who have been entering the medical and legal professions in roughly equal numbers with men for most of that time, do not have equality of opportunity with men and do not reach the same professional heights. If Muslims have been in this country in significant numbers for thirty years, could they not argue that they have not reached equality with other groups in the population? And is it not legitimate for Muslims to argue that part of that rests on religious intolerance, which is one facet of racial intolerance, but can be so conveniently disguised? And isn't the state a party to that?

Of course they could, and often do. But the argument in the chattering classes is that the Muslims have got it wrong. What is wrong with Islam is that it is 'fundamentalist', that it discriminates against women, that the killing of animals in the prescribed way is barbaric, that Muslims are violent . . . and I could cite more and more examples from the popular and not-so-popular press. Let us have a look at some of these ideas.

First, Islam is fundamentalist. Well, it is true to say that there is a large tranche of Muslims who are what western people would describe as fundamentalist. They believe in an unchanging law, a law that is true as a whole, and some believe in the innate superiority of Islam over all other faiths, to the extent – though relatively limited – of persecuting those of other faiths in countries which are con- trolled by Islamic rulers. However, history also demonstrates that Muslim rulers have been more tolerant of minorities than Christian rulers. And if there are Muslim fundamentalists, it is equally true that there are Christian fundamentalists in abundance throughout the world, and most significantly in the United States and Ireland, though of very different breeds.

Nor is any other religious group exempt from fundamentalism. There is the political and religious fundamentalism of the Israeli Gush Emunim and other Jewish groups in Israel and the US. That variety of fundamentalism leads to a policy which regards all non-Jews as inferior, and it is at least in part based on a view that the land – the 'Biblical' land of Judea and Samaria – belongs only and historically to Jews, whoever else is there at the time. Again, there is the religious and political fundamentalism of Sikhs and Hindus in conflict in India, and there is growing tension between what is seen as religious and what can be perceived as political when, for so many fundamentalists, the two are indistinguishable and the political policies are God's will.

Yet Muslims are attacked more than most for their fundamentalist views. Partly, in this country and the US, that is because of the Rushdie affair. Yet in a sense the reaction to the Ayatollah's ban on the book and the death threat to Rushdie himself constituted a failure on the part of white liberals to understand what was going on and a deep revulsion (particularly amongst journalists) to the idea that there should be censorship. The liberal left got caught up in knots. The Ayatollah was being a fundamentalist, and was impinging on the freedoms of the rest of the world. Therefore he was bad. Yet to speak out against the death threat and in support of Rushdie was not only to take some personal risk (certainly for publishers and booksellers), but also to suggest a form of racism on the part of liberals: if the Ayatollah was wrong, and he was a Muslim leader, and other Muslims were following him, then Islam itself was bad and all Muslims were suspect.

Liberal after liberal spoke out against the Ayatollah, and in my view they were right to condemn the death threat and to question censorship for whatever reason. But those same liberal thinkers were quick neither to advocate the abolition of the blasphemy legislation in this country (legislation which protects only Christianity), nor to support a new criminal offence of causing offence to religious groupings of whatever kind. In other words, precisely those groups who most condemned the death threat, and accused Islam of fundamentalism, recognised and to some extent protected and supported the status quo of legislation, vastly outdated, which protects only Christianity. Even if that was not a conscious piece of religious triumphalism (because most of those who held that position were not religious in any sense), it was nevertheless an acceptance that Christianity is the religion of our country and that no other religion has any status.

Let us move on to other accusations made against Islam. It discriminates against women. Indeed it does. So does orthodox Judaism, and most of Eastern Christianity. So does Western Christianity, at least in so far as it restricts the roles that women can fill in the church, and in England the established Church has only recently ordained women to the priesthood. Again, it is alleged that traditional Islam has tended to promote a less academic, less full education for girls. But so has traditional Catholicism and traditional Greek orthodoxy. Nor is Sikhism immune from this behaviour, nor Hinduism. Indeed, part of the discrimination against women is not religious but cultural, though formed by religious thought, particularly emanating from the Indian sub-continent; and it has to be said that under Islamic law, as under Jewish law, women did at least have a status, unlike their position under Christian canon law, where they were chattels, and of little value.

It is important to make this clear. Those who most criticise Islam see this discrimination as its worst feature. Yet they fail to see that their own religion, or the religion from which their families came, has been just as discriminatory, and that it is the effect of the loosening of religious control and the gaining in ground of secularism which has most influenced the change within Europe and the US. This is not to suggest that I would defend the anti-feminist position of many Muslims and many orthodox Jews. Of course I would not, but it helps to see these things in perspective, and to realise that the weapons used against religious groups are often tainted by ignorance as well as prejudice, ignorance of one's own tradition as much as of the other.

Anti-Islamic feeling in particular is caught up in a mixture of race hatred and religious suspicion. In the West, where religion and ethnicity are seen as two very different things, the idea that one's religious grouping is a cultural definition is very foreign. The idea that belief is less important than action, and that one is judged by one's actions and observance of religious law, is anathema to those who believe that salvation comes through faith as well as, and in precedence to, acts.

Indeed, one of the reasons why tolerance is difficult in its true sense for many Christians is that they have failed to see what it is they are being asked to be tolerant of. It is not of a different faith *per se*, though that is part of it. It is of cultural definitions, cultural allegiances that are expressed by religious ritual, as well as profound religious faith. It is of a sense of peoplehood, hard for Christians in particular to understand, unless they are a minority group or have a strong ethnic background as Armenian Christians do. However, Islam, Judaism, Sikhism, Hinduism, particularly in the West, are defined by a mixture of a sense of allegiance to a people, however ill defined, and an allegiance to a set of religious and cultural practices. Although many have strong religious beliefs as well, that comes second for the majority. It is the self-definition as part of a clear minority group with its own practices which is overwhelmingly the most important factor. It is questions about being absorbed into the mass, assimilating, losing cultural identity, losing religious identity, which most concern many of these groups. It is fear of intermarriage, of loss of religious identity of children, loss of values that keep the communities together, and that can be both enriching and suffocating for the next generation.

What we need to look at is how religious groups, both those which are relative newcomers, and the traditional grouping of the dominant and politically powerful Church of England, can be tolerant of others, comfortable within themselves, and ultimately permissive towards their own members as well as supplying a strong foundation in religious and cultural traditions.

Several things need to be achieved for that to happen. First, on the part of the state there needs to be a change of heart about the predominantly Christian thrust of education legislation when the majority of the population does not go to church, and there are significant numbers of non-Christian minorities in the society. That recognition in itself, freely given, would allow a sense of acceptance to percolate through to the Islamic, Sikh, Hindu and Jewish communities. Then, secondly, there is a need for those communities themselves to be more forthcoming in talking to each other and in talking to Christian groups: here, basic knowledge and understanding are often sadly lacking, so that, for instance, medical staff who are wholly well disposed to providing care sensitive to religious and cultural needs do not know what ought to be done, and are hampered by a lack of willingness on the parts of minority religious groupings to come and speak to them about different requirements. Then there is a need for the language of tolerance, heard in almost all the religious groupings, to be put into practice. That can only happen, as with feminism, by giving up space, and what that means is that Christians, bishops of the Church of England, must give up space in the House of Lords for the religious leaders of other faiths. And they must do so on principle. It also means that the Church of England must campaign hard for multicultural religious education in schools, and resist religious indoctrination in schools. It means that religious leaders must talk less about Christian values, and more about neutral words appreciated by members of all faiths – words like 'community', which are often better understood by members of other faiths than by Anglicans. It means having multi-faith institutions for care, where religious figures of all persuasions have the right to enter and give comfort to patients. Chaplains have begun to do well in that regard, and some, such as Mark Cobb at Derby,[4] have taken an important lead. But it is still the case at conferences on spiritual care that it is considered legitimate to talk as if Christian spirituality were the only kind of spirituality. In fact, there is spirituality in all faiths, and public institutions give out the wrong messages if they imply otherwise.

It also means education in multiculturalism, with all its attendant difficulties. It means the Department for Education and Employment doing a quick turnaround and insisting on multicultural education in schools as part of the national curriculum, at least in part in religious studies, and at least in part in any work on citizenship. That should happen not only for the clear virtues multiculturalism has as a concept, but also because of the message of tolerance it proclaims in itself. It means those religious groups which proselytise realising that that very activity is offensive, and that there needs to be a theological change of heart, recognising as equal but different the faiths of other people, and no longer trying to convert them to one's own faith on the grounds that it is better, or promises salvation, or whatever.

For Christians, that is particularly hard to do. Yet there was a brave attempt to regard Jews as people not to be proselytised at the last Lambeth conference, with a moving and profound speech by the Bishop of Oxford arguing for Jews to be 'off limits'.[5] What needs to be taken on board is whether those other religions have equality with one's own or not. If the answer is yes, then proselytising ceases as of right. If the answer is no, then the limit of tolerance has been reached, and the truth of the matter is that the religion is not tolerant in its true sense. At that point we touch on a theological agenda beyond my scope here, but suffice it to say that the line lies there, and it is in the area of conversion activity, in the area of stated claims to salvation to the exclusion of others, and in the quest for religious dominance of education and the provision of goods and services, that the line lies.

And, as we move nearer the millennium, far away from my

expectations, we are becoming a less tolerant, more triumphalist, less accepting, more condemnatory society. And the approach of the millennium is the approach of an intolerant religious field in the midst of political turmoil where religion is playing a major part in defining what side people fight on, and where their allegiances lie. For the UK to become genuinely tolerant, religiously speaking, would therefore require major shifts in thinking about immigration in general and asylum legislation in particular, shifts in thinking about education in general and religious worship in schools in particular. It would require the Church of England to move over to allow space in representative terms to other faiths, and to campaign for voluntary aided status for Muslim schools, or the abolition of the lot. And that would only be the beginning, setting out that well-known but as yet non-existent level playing field on which the game could be played fairly.

So religious toleration is feasible, certainly, but as things stand at present it is not very likely, unless people of good will – people of all faiths and of none – press for recognition of other faiths in education, in representation in Parliament, and in understanding of what causes offence.

Notes

1. Dipak Nandy, 'Race as Politics', in *Towards an Open Society*, London, Pemberton Books, 1971.
2. A. J. Sherman, *Island Refuge – Britain and Refugees from the Third Reich 1933–1939*, London, Frank Cass, 1994.
3. In January 1998, subsequent to the delivery of this lecture, the Secretary of State for Education approved grant-maintained status for two Muslim primary schools.
4. Mark Cobb organised the highly successful first conference on spiritual care in health in Derby in 1995.
5. The document was entitled 'The Truth Shall Make You Free' (London, Anglican Consultative Council, 1988) and the Bishop of Oxford played a large part in its drafting, as well as speaking to it at the Lambeth Conference 1988.

Chapter 9

Toleration and the goods of conflict
Alasdair MacIntyre

What questions should we ask?

When ought we to be intolerant and why? I pose this question in the first instance as one concerning the ethics of conversation and, more particularly, the ethics of one particular kind of conversation. That kind of conversation occurs when a group of individuals enquire together about how it would be best for them to act, so that some good can be achieved or some evil avoided, where that good is both an individual and a common good – the good of this or that household or neighbourhood, this or that workplace or school or clinic, this or that orchestra or laboratory or chess or football club. The central aim of this type of conversation is to arrive at as large a measure as possible of agreement that will issue in effective practical decision-making. But it cannot achieve this central aim unless it also achieves two subsidiary aims: that of enabling those who participate in it both to give voice to their own concerns and to understand those of others, and by so doing that of framing and cataloguing the best reasons for and against each alternative course of action.

Such conversations from time to time are a feature of any flourishing form of everyday social life. They are also characteristically and not surprisingly scenes of conflict. For they are most needed when significantly different alternative possibilities in its immediate future have opened up for some particular group and when there are at least *prima facie* good reasons for different and incompatible courses of action. And just this type of occasion is apt to elicit differences between individuals concerning their larger conceptions of their individual and common goods that had not hitherto been articulated. Disagreements over particular issues always may and sometimes do turn out to be rooted in more systematic disagreements.

Conflict is therefore as integral to the life of such groups as conversation. And in order for such a group to flourish it must be able to manage its conflicts, so that neither of two evils befalls it. The first of these is the evil of suppression, of thinking that one has avoided conflict by somehow or other depriving one party to it of the means for expressing its attitudes, concerns and arguments. The other is the evil of disruption, of the kind of disagreement and the modes of expression of disagreement which destroy the possibility of arriving at the degree and kind of consensus necessary for effective shared decision-making. Sometimes at least one of these evils is produced by those who are attempting to avoid the other. It is on occasion the prospect of disruption that leads to suppression. And it is sometimes the fear of suppression that engenders disruptive attitudes.

It is in this kind of local context where, although the conversation may be conducted in a variety of ways, it cannot but involve face-to-face encounters, that certain issues of toleration arise. For, when we are involved in debate with those who hold conflicting points of view, we may take any of four distinct attitudes to the utterances of others. We may welcome them as either reinforcing our own conclusions or as assisting in the reformulation or revision of those conclusions. Or we may welcome them equally as contributing to sharp, but constructive disagreement, by providing compelling reasons for adopting some point of view other than and incompatible with our own. In both these types of case we treat the utterances as contributing in a co-operative way to the achievement of the shared goods of conversational enquiry. In a third type of case we may regard the utterance as not so contributing, but as still requiring a reasonable answer, in order to convince the utterer, if possible, that, for example, the difficulty that she or he envisages is not going to arise or that the view expressed rests on some easily corrigible misinformation or misunderstanding. But there is also a fourth type of utterance to which the only appropriate response is to exclude the speaker temporarily or permanently from discussion. This is not primarily a matter of suppressing the expression of some point of view within the debate. It is a matter of expelling someone from the debate. Either the matter or the manner – or both – of her or his utterance has been taken to disqualify the speaker as a participant. What she or he said or how she or he said it has destroyed her or his conversational standing. The utterance is intolerable.

My initial questions are: what is the line to be drawn that divides this fourth type of utterance from the other three? That is to say, what is the difference between justified intolerance and unjustified suppression? Who is to draw that line? And, when drawn, how is it to be enforced as a norm governing this kind of conversation? But before I can fruitfully ask these questions, I need to make three remarks. The first is that answers to these questions already inform, sometimes explicitly, often implicitly, the life of every social group. In practice every group sets a limit to its tolerance and in one way or another enforces that limit. My enquiry therefore takes it for granted that in the course of our disagreements and conflicts we are going to be intolerant and that the only questions are of what, of whom, and why. Secondly, we should note that disagreement and conflict occur not only within the kind of group that I have described, but also between groups. Some particular group with a well-worked-out conception of the goods to be achieved in its particular arenas of activity always may and often does encounter another such group whose conception of the goods to be conceived differs in important respects from its own. Where within each group rival arguments had proceeded from some set of more or less agreed premises and presupposed a shared understanding of the concepts involved, now in the debate between groups each has to attempt to find some ultimate ground to which both may appeal and, in so doing, to re-examine the concepts upon which they have been relying. In the exchanges between such groups the same fourfold classification of utterances that applied to debate within groups will find application. So that once again the question will arise: what kinds of utterance, if any, ought to be found intolerable?

Secondly, it is in important part through disagreement and conflict that the common life of such groups is enriched. For it is only through disagreement and conflict, only through aiming at conclusions that emerge from being tested by the most powerful counter-arguments available, that such groups are able to embody in their shared lives the rational pursuit and achievement of the relevant goods. Therefore when we evaluate the argumentative contributions to some ongoing debate within a group in whose life we participate, we should do so with an eye to how far they do or do not contribute to achieving the goods of conflict. So what is to be treated as intolerable is anything the toleration of which would tend to frustrate or prevent the achievement of those goods. Particular practices of or proposals for the practice of toleration can only be adequately evaluated from within the context of conflict. And the line between what we are prepared to tolerate and what we refuse to tolerate always partially defines our stance in some set of conflicts.

Locke's proposals concerning toleration and the state

In trying to answer these questions about the relationship between the goods of conflict and toleration in the context of certain kinds of conversation, what can we learn from the classical texts on toleration? Here I want to distinguish between what is to be learned from Locke and what is to be learned from Mill.[1] And I shall argue that we ought to agree with at least some of Locke's conclusions – or rather perhaps with conclusions drawn from lines of thought initiated by Locke, while deriving those conclusions from premises of a very different kind from Locke's, but that in Mill's case we should assent to some of his premises, while drawing very different conclusions. I begin with Locke.

It is a commonplace that what are now treated as the classical texts on toleration for the most part have as their context those seventeenth- and eighteenth-century European conflicts in which what was at stake was, on the one hand the relationship between groups that embraced a variety of incompatible versions of the Christian religion, and the power and authority of the state on the other. The single most influential position that emerged from those texts was that towards which Locke had moved as his thoughts on these issues developed: it is the function and duty of the magistrate to promote the security, order and harmony of a people, but not to attempt to regulate or even to influence their beliefs, except when, as in the case, on Locke's view, of Roman Catholics and atheists, religious belief itself or the lack of it threatens such security, order and harmony.

Locke's arguments exhibited a certain tension in his attitudes. On the one hand he seems to have held that genuine belief, interior assent, cannot be commanded, that coercion can produce at most the outward appearance of conformity. No one, he says, is able to 'command his own understanding or positively determine today what opinion he will be of tomorrow', and therefore no one can give another power 'over that over which he has no power himself'.[2] So he draws a conclusion about religious belief from the nature of belief as such. On the other hand, when Locke had to reply to Jonas Proast's thesis that a moderate use of coercive power could in fact induce someone to consider arguments to which they would not otherwise have attended with care, Locke responded that we do not have sufficiently good reasons for asserting any one particular set of religious doctrines to justify us in using the power of the state on its behalf.[3] And in so saying he seems to distinguish religious beliefs from other types of belief.

Each of these arguments anticipates a strain in subsequent liberal thought about toleration. On the one hand, so far as possible individuals are to be left alone to make up their own minds, free from interference by the prescriptions of political or religious authority. Each individual cannot but be the sole authority on how things appear to her or him to be and on her or his consequent beliefs. And this is true of all beliefs, not just of religious beliefs or of beliefs about the nature of the human good. On the other hand, religious beliefs and, more generally, beliefs about the nature of the human good are to be treated as unlike other beliefs in that they are indefinitely contestable. And for this reason their propagation and influence are to be subject to restriction in a way that other beliefs are not. The state may justifiably mandate curricula in the natural sciences by which belief in the theory of evolution by natural selection is inculcated. But it may not justifiably mandate curricula by which belief in the divine creation of the universe is inculcated. For on questions of religion and more generally on questions concerning the human good the state is to be neutral as between different points of view.

Toleration is therefore to be extended to the exponents of any and every point of view, provided only that they do not threaten the security, order and harmony of society. Not only may the state not attempt to impose any one view, but no one else may either. The word 'impose' is important here. What is excluded is coercion, especially coercive violence or the threat of coercive violence. But no limit, or almost no limit, is placed on the means of persuasion that may otherwise be allowed. Indeed the freedom extended to religious and other groups commonly includes a freedom to use whatever means of persuasion they choose, once again provided only that they do not threaten society's security, order and harmony.

Locke himself of course, like those later liberals who developed and to some degree transformed his thought, was a participant in those very same conflicts which he proposed to resolve by, among other things, the legislative enforcement of toleration. That legislative enforcement was the work of what had first been a contending and then became a victorious party in the seventeenth-century conflicts over religion. And the modern state which originated as the instrument of that victorious party's purposes was itself never neutral in the conflicts that continued to divide the society over which it presided. Here we need only note that the conceptions which the state principally championed were particular and highly contestable conceptions of liberty and of property and of the relationship between them – conceptions which of course changed over time – and that it systematically favoured those groups and parties whose understanding of the human good was consistent with the state's own conceptions of liberty and property, and systematically disfavoured those whose understandings were antagonistic to the state. But, having noted that the modern state is never merely a neutral arbiter of conflicts, but is always to some degree itself a party to social conflict, and that it acts in the interests of particular and highly contestable conceptions of liberty and property, we need also to remember how very different our present condition is from that of the eighteenth century, and this in at least three respects.

The nature and values of the contemporary state

What are the relevant differences? First, in many areas of the West politics has been successfully secularised and the political importance of religion greatly diminished. There are of course still large parts of the world in which it is the persecution of religious believers by those invested with state power that makes issues of toleration so urgent. But for the advanced modernity of the West it is only relatively rarely that such issues concern religion. Sometimes of course they do, and not unimportantly, especially when they concern the rights of parents to bring up their children according to the tenets of some particular religion. But even here we will do well to extend our discussion more widely, so that from this point on I will speak only of rival conceptions of the human good, including religious conceptions under this heading.

Secondly, the contemporary state has become very different from the eighteenth-century state, and this in obvious ways. The scope of its activities has been greatly enlarged as has the effect of those activities on the economy. The number, size and variety of its agencies have increased enormously. The complexity of its legislation, its tax codes and its administrative regulations are such that to grasp their detail is now generally beyond the reach of ordinary citizens, a fact whose significance it is difficult to over-rate. And, while the modern state always was more and other than a set of instrumental means to realise the purposes of those who had achieved control of its mechanisms, it has become more and more a set of institutions which have their own values.

Thirdly, the contemporary state is to a remarkable degree united in an indissoluble partnership with the national and international market. It relies upon the operations of those markets for the material resources which taxation affords. And those markets rely on it for the provision of that social and legal framework without which they could not enjoy the stability that they need. It is true that there are often minor confrontations between this or that agency of government and the agents of this or that aspect of market operations. And it is true that there are ongoing ideological debates about where the boundaries between public and government, corporate activity and private corporate activity, are to be drawn. But the agreements underlying those conflicts and the shared presuppositions of those debates reflect the common needs of state and market for capital formation, for economic growth and for an adequately trained but disposable labour force, whose members are also compliant consumers and law-abiding citizens.

Let us then think of the contemporary state and the contemporary national economy as a huge, single, complex, heterogeneous, immensely powerful something or other, noting that it gives expression to both its power and its values in two very different ways. On the one hand there is the mask that it wears in all those everyday transactions in which individuals and groups are compelled to deal with a heterogeneous range of public and private corporate agencies: paying their taxes, applying for employment and welfare, buying a house, being arrested, getting an education. Here, what individuals and groups encounter in the first instance is the administrative application of rules to instances. Those rules are part of those codes of laws and regulations whose complexity makes them more or less inaccessible to the vast majority of individuals and groups. If individuals or groups are to question the application of the rules in their particular case, they generally therefore have to put themselves into the hands of experts. If they go further and try to put the rules in question, they find themselves able to do so effectively only in so far as they learn how to employ the same idioms and types of argument with which the representatives of state and market justify their rules and their decisions. The concepts central to those idioms and arguments are those of *utility* and of *rights*.

Consider how such justificatory argument proceeds through three stages. There are first of all those cost-benefit analyses designed to provide good reasons for preferring one set of decision-making procedures or one policy alternative to another. In constructing such analyses there are always questions of whose preferences are to be included in the analyses, of what time scale it is over which costs and benefits are to be measured, and of who is to decide the answers to the first two questions. And the answers to these questions determine where power lies. Next a second type of argument has to be advanced, which proceeds by first identifying those individuals and groups who may have grounds for claiming that to maximise utility in accordance with the conclusions of the cost-benefit analysis will be to violate some right of theirs, and then enquiring what grounds there are for agreeing with their claim. What the first and second types of argument yield are conclusions which in a third type of argument have to be weighed against one another to provide an answer to the question: what weight in this particular context is to be given to the conclusions concerning the rights of those involved, and what weight to the conclusions concerning what course of action will maximise the relevant utilities? How is the one set of considerations to be balanced against the other?

The metaphors of weighing and balancing are indispensable to this stage of argument. But what their use obscures is a salient fact: there are no scales. That is, not only is there no rationally justifiable general rule by which claims about utilities can be evaluated as over-riding or as failing to over-ride claims about rights, but in each particular context what decides how such claims will be adjudicated will always depend upon who it is that in that particular context has the power to adjudicate, and how this power to adjudicate is related to the distribution of economic, political and social power more generally. But this is not the only rhetorical mode in which state and market present themselves.

For they wear quite another mask and speak with quite another voice when they justify their policies and actions in their role as custodians of society's values, presenting the state as the guardian of the nation's ideals and the caretaker of its heritage, and the market as the institutionalised expression of its liberties. It is in this guise that the state from time to time invites us to die on its behalf and that the market fosters through its advertising agencies fantasies about well-being. This type of rhetoric relies not on the idioms of utility and rights, but on the persuasive definition and redefinition of such terms as 'liberty', 'democracy', 'free market', and the like. And it is a prerequisite for achieving certain kinds of status within the apparatus of state and market that one should be able to move effectively between the one rhetorical mode and the other.

What the modes of justification employed in and on behalf of the activities of state and market cannot give expression to are the values that inform just those ongoing argumentative conversations through which members of local communities try to achieve their goods and their good. The values of state and market are not only different from, but on many types of occasion incompatible with, the values of such local community. For the former, decision-making is arrived at by a summing of preferences and by a series of trade-offs, in which whose preferences are summed and what is traded off against what depends upon the political and economic bargaining power of the representatives of contending interests. For the latter, a shared understanding of the common good of the relevant type of activity or sets of activities provides a standard independent of preferences and interests, one by reference to which individual preferences and group interests are to be evaluated. For the former there is no consideration that may not under certain circumstances be outweighed by some other consideration. For the latter, there are conclusive considerations, those that refer us to goods that cannot be sacrificed or foregone without rendering the activity in which the community is engaged pointless. For the former, a gift for flexibility and compromise, for knowing when and how to exchange one set of principles for another, is accounted a central political virtue. For the latter, a certain moral intransigence of a kind that is apt to prevent success in the larger worlds of the state and the market economy is accounted among the political virtues.

Toleration and the contemporary state

It is a consequence of these features of the social life of advanced modernity that there is always tension and sometimes conflict between the demands of state and market on the one hand and the requirements of rational local community on the other. Those who value rational local communal enterprise are therefore wise to order their relationships with state and market so that, as far as possible, they remain able to draw upon those resources that can only be secured from state and market, while preserving their own self-sufficiency, their self-reliance, and their freedom from constraint by either. They must treat the agencies of the state with unremitting suspicion.

So by a very different route we have arrived at very much the same conclusion as that reached both by classical liberals and by modern liberals: the state must not be allowed to impose any one particular conception of the human good or identify some one such conception with its own interests and causes. It must afford tolerance to a diversity of standpoints. But liberals generally have arrived at these conclusions because they believe either that the state ought to be neutral between different rival conceptions of the good or that states ought actively to promote the liberty and autonomy of individuals in making their own choices. I have argued by contrast first that the contemporary state is not and cannot be evaluatively neutral, and secondly that it is just because of the ways in which the state is not evaluatively neutral that it cannot generally be trusted to promote any worthwhile set of values, including those of autonomy and liberty.

What has most often been feared in the past was that the state, by favouring one point of view exclusively, would damage the interests of those who gave their allegiance to other standpoints. The harm done by the legally sanctioned hegemony of an established church would be a harm done to dissenters and to the liberty to dissent. But although this kind of harm is still to be feared, grave harm would also be done to the cause of those whose point of view the state had made its own. For the contemporary state could not adopt a point of view on the human good as its own without to a significant degree distorting, degrading and discrediting that point of view. It would put those values to the service of its own political and economic power and so degrade and discredit them. The principal harm that was done by the hegemony accorded to the Roman Catholic Church by regimes as different as those of Franco's Spain and De Valera's Ireland was after all to the Roman Catholic religion.

I have now given a partial and negative answer to one of my initial questions. Whoever is to draw the line between those points of view concerning the human good whose expression is to be tolerated and those points of view whose expression is not to be tolerated, it should not be the agencies of the state. It is very much to be desired that those agencies should provide for the equal protection of all the state's subjects from a wide variety of harms, and that this protection should be characterised so that it preserves an ostensible neutrality on the part of the state. Even although that neutrality is never real, it is an important fiction, and those of us who recognise its importance as well as its fictional character will agree with liberals in upholding a certain range of civil liberties.

The exclusions and intolerances necessary for rational communal dialogue

The state, however, must not be allowed to impose constraints that would prevent local groups from ordering their own conversations concerning their common goods as practically rational dialogue. And the conditions for promoting and maintaining such practically rational dialogue require certain local exclusions and intolerances. Consider five such conditions.

The first concerns *who* is to participate in the conversation. If some group aiming at a common good is engaged in practically rational conversation aimed at reaching a decision that will be genuinely its own decision, it must ensure that all its members are able to voice their concerns and evaluate the arguments that are advanced, so that what is arrived at is the reality and not merely the appearance of consensus. But it must also ensure that those with irrelevant or conflicting aims do not subvert their shared enquiry. So, for example, in discussion designed to identify how the goods of health are to be defined concretely for some particular community with a particular age distribution and a particular set of threats to its health, the contribution of physicians, nurses, therapists of various kinds, actual and potential patients and those who have responsibility for children or for the aged are all germane to the enquiry, while those of the representatives of insurance companies or of bureaucratic managers of health-care organisations are not. The latter do indeed have an interest in how the goods of health are defined, but the kind of interest that should render them not participants in this discussion, but objects of suspicion and candidates for exclusion.

Of course once the members of a given community have decided how the goods of health are to be defined correctly for them in their circumstances, they themselves must then face the further question of how much of their resources they are able and prepared to make available to achieve those goods, what other types of good they will consequently be unable to achieve and how they should use those resources as efficiently as possible. And at this later stage of discussion some kinds of contribution that were irrelevant or even corrupting at an earlier stage may well become relevant.

Let me put this point in another way. The more open a discussion is to anyone and everyone, so that multifarious interests of indefinitely many kinds may find expression, and there are few, if any, widely shared presuppositions, then that discussion can only have a direction and an ordered agenda that will issue in the making of decisions if such a direction and agenda, and the form of decision-making, are imposed upon the discussion by those with the power so to impose. That power in the liberal democracies of advanced modernity rests with the elites of the political parties and of the mass media and it is they who largely decide the direction of discussion and its agenda, so determining not what the public chooses, but what the alternatives are between which public choices are made.

If the participants themselves are not only to engage in but to control the direction of genuinely rational discussion that determines practical outcomes, there has to be some large measure of initial agreement about what it is that needs to be decided, about what the standards are by which better reasons for decision and action are to be discriminated from worse, and about what goods are at stake. The rational resolution of disagreement thus requires some measure of prior agreement, agreement which can itself always be put in question, if there turns out to be good reason to question it. And the initial agreement that is needed can only be secured by exclusions, exclusions that must themselves be agreed and be open to question.

Secondly, rational discussion and enquiry in which all the relevant voices are to be heard is incompatible with certain modes of expression. Threatening and insulting utterance, utterance that brings certain others in the discussion into contempt or makes them feel insecure, that addresses their motives, their persons, their ethnic characteristics or their gender, rather than their arguments or their conclusions, are so much a violation of the norms of rational discussion that they should be treated as a kind of self-expulsion from the discussion, an expression of a will to be expelled. The group should consent to and enforce this self-imposed withdrawal, perhaps temporarily. Local rationality mandates local intolerance.

To this it will be replied that I seem to have an absurdly unrealistic and sterile view of how local communal debate proceeds when it is genuinely informed by its members' concerns. Jokes, mockery and indignation are after all only a few of the forms taken by the rhetoric of reason-informed passion, and reason-informed passion is what moves those who participate in such debate. How then are we to draw a line between jokes and insults, between legitimate mockery of a view and illegitimate mockery of those who hold that view? How can we possibly legislate against the clever sneer and the subtle act of condescension?

The answer is that rationality compels us to admit the force of both sets of considerations and that there can indeed be no hard and fast rule by which such a line can be drawn. What is required is the exercise of judgement and the cultivation of those virtues necessary for the exercise of judgement. That the members of a rational community have to educate themselves and each other into these and other virtues, and that such an education takes time, draws our attention to the fact that any particular community that exhibits rationality does so as a result only of an extended self-education into the virtues of practical rationality and that any particular community will have made more or less progress in this education. A capacity for judgement has to emerge. We have to learn how to be rationally intolerant of certain kinds of utterance.

To these already catalogued exclusions and intolerances we need to add another. It is a condition of rational discussion and enquiry that certain questions should be understood by the participants to have been settled conclusively. More than this, an insistence that certain kinds of question remain open may be a sign of a type of character that disqualifies those who possess it from further participation in discussion. Consider first an absurd example. Dr Rumpelstiltskin is an apparently intelligent and well-informed person. He has a doctorate in the humanities from a leading university. His range of opinions resembles those of other such persons, with one notable exception: he is deeply and passionately convinced of the truth of the phlogiston theory of combustion. He publishes at his own expense pamphlets denouncing Priestley and Lavoisier for having diverted chemistry from its true course. He advances explanations for their successes, explanations that display a certain ingenuity, but are likely to convince only those who are almost completely ignorant of chemistry. How do we in fact treat such as Rumpelstiltskin?

The answer is that we all of us tacitly agree to silence him by ignoring him, and among other measures that we take we exclude him from any discussion in which the truth or otherwise of particular chemical theories is taken in any way seriously. The papers that he prepares for delivery at scientific meetings are never accepted. His letters to journals and newspapers go unpublished. At public lectures, once the chair knows who he is, he is deliberately ignored at question time. His pamphlets are unread, except as jokes. But are we prepared to allow Rumpelstiltskin to teach in schools or colleges subjects other than chemistry – ancient history, say?

No one reasonable will say 'No' to this, unless it is discovered that his prestige with his students in his ancient history classes may be making some of them take his views on chemistry seriously, so that some students who would otherwise have chosen to take classes in chemistry elect other alternatives to their own detriment. This would certainly provide some grounds for denying Rumpelstiltskin a position as a teacher. How strong these grounds would be taken to be would, I suggest, be very generally a matter of how great the influence on his students was. But there would be some degree of influence that would make it appropriate no longer to employ him as a teacher, to exclude his views and with them him not only from the scientific but also from the larger academic community. That is, our position on such as Rumpelstiltskin is in fact that we do nothing to hinder the expression of their views, so

long as we are assured that no one gives them serious consideration.

Consider now what Mill asserts in Chapter 2 of *On Liberty* (the
chapter entitled 'Of the Liberty of Thought and Discussion'), namely
that we should not only tolerate but also welcome the expression of
all and any opinions that deviate from whatever in a particular society
is taken to be the accepted norm. 'If all mankind minus one were of
one opinion, and only one person were of the contrary opinion,
mankind would be no more justified in silencing that one person,
than he, if he had the power, would be justified in silencing
mankind.'[4] Mill, we should remind ourselves, was envisaging the
silencing of opinions by government, government which had made
itself the instrument of public opinion, of what Mill calls 'the general
intolerance of the public'. And I have already agreed that we ought
not to allow government – or at least the governments of modern
states – to suppress opinions. But what I hope the example of the
fictitious Dr Rumpelstiltskin shows is that we do not have to invoke
the powers of government to silence the expression of opinions.
They can be and often are effectively silenced at a range of local levels
by the tacit or even explicit agreement of the relevant communities.
It is true that what is involved here is not that 'general intolerance of
public opinion' which Mill had in mind. But it is a form of
suppression that is flagrantly at odds with Mill's ringing and un-
qualified declarations.

What I am suggesting here is that there is a class of opinions which
many of us, liberals and non-liberals alike, agree in exempting from
Mill's ban on suppression, although often without acknowledging
that we do so. And our reason for disagreeing with Mill is that we
take it not to be true of this class of opinions that its suppression
involves what Mill took to be 'the peculiar evil' of suppression, that:

> it is robbing the human race; posterity as well as the existing
> generation; those who dissent from the opinion, still more than
> those who hold it. If the opinion is right, they are deprived of the
> opportunity of exchanging error for truth: if wrong, they lose, what is
> almost as great a benefit, the clearer perception and livelier impression
> of truth, produced by its collision with error'.[5]

What is deeply implausible in this is the suggestion that the serious reassertion of the phlogiston theory of combustion in any mode whatsoever could do anything to produce a 'clearer perception and livelier impression' of those truths of modern chemistry that displaced it two hundred years ago.

To this it may be said that it is the example that is misleading and that it is significant that I have employed a fictitious example. No one does in fact now hold, because no one could now hold, the phlogiston theory of combustion. And more generally the class of opinions that would provide counter-examples to Mill's generalisation is empty. Moreover, if such opinions were held, their expression would be self-discrediting. Their suppression is either unnecessary or pointless. There are, however, real-life examples of scientific opinions uncomfortably close to Rumpelstiltskin's that have flourished in some quarters very recently – I have in mind not only the beliefs of members of Flat Earth Societies, but also some kinds of rejection of Darwinism. But the type of example that it is most important to consider as a possible counter-example to Mill's claims is of a different kind.

Consider the assertion and the attempted justifications of the assertion that the Holocaust – the intended and to a horrifying extent achieved destruction of the Jewish people by those acting under the orders of Hitler and Himmler or collaborating with them, and with it the intended and to a horrifying extent achieved destruction of the Romany people, the gypsies – never happened and that the belief that it happened is a fabrication of anti-Nazi propaganda. How should we stand on the freedom to express this opinion?

So far as the intervention of government is concerned, we have the opposing examples of the United States and of Germany. In the United States twentieth-century interpretations of the First Amendment have made it quite clear that the liberty to express this opinion, like the liberty to express any other opinion, has to be guaranteed by the state. It would indeed be open to a university to deny an appointment in, say, modern German history to someone holding this opinion, on the grounds that it exhibited gross incompetence in the evaluation of evidence. But to deny some individual well qualified in some other field, in one of the natural or applied sciences, say, a professorial appointment just because he or she held and expressed this opinion, and just because his or her holding a professorial appointment enhanced the credibility of this opinion among certain types of people, would be an infringement of that individual's First Amendment rights. In Germany, by contrast, the utterance of this opinion is, I understand, a punishable crime. How are we to decide between these rival views?

Two features of the denial of the Holocaust are relevant to answering this question. First of all, the denial of the Holocaust is certainly an intervention in the debates between the protagonists of different and rival conceptions of the human good. For what some particular conception of the human good amounts to is always a matter in part of what allegiance to it amounts to or would amount to in practice. What would it be like to live in a society informed by this particular conception? It is not of course a conclusive objection to a particular conception of the human good that those whose practice has been directed to it as their supreme end have in fact been guilty of many and great evils. For the source of those evils may not have been in that conception of the good, but rather in its distortion or in the imperfections of its realisation, or in some contingent features of the history of its adherents that are only related *per accidens* to that conception. Nonetheless the history of how some particular conception of the human good has been embodied in practice is always of great relevance in evaluating it. And for anyone who is concerned to evaluate all those conceptions of the human good that have played a central part in European history – those of Catholic Christianity, of different types of Protestant Christianity, of a variety of doctrines and movements stemming from or reacting to the Enlightenment – the relationship of their history to the history of European anti-Semitism has to be of immense importance.

It follows that were the state to proscribe and punish utterances that afford expression to a denial of the Holocaust, the state would be actively intervening in the debates between protagonists of rival conceptions of the human good. And it was my conclusion earlier that such interventions by the state are bound to be pernicious. I am therefore bound to side with the law of the United States rather than that of Germany; as I do. But it does not follow that utterances that afford expression to a denial of the Holocaust ought to be tolerated generally. Why not?

Local communities engaged in systematic conversation about their own good have to treat certain questions as already decided. And among these by now are questions about the evils of anti-Semitism. Indeed the poisons of anti-Semitism are such that no conception of the human good can be treated as rationally defensible whose defenders cannot show not only how allegiance to it can be dissociated from anti-Semitism, but also how it can provide or acquire resources for neutralising those poisons. And that can be done only by those who recognise the facts of the Holocaust. I do not mean by this that there are not many other facts that also need to be recognised. But I take the facts about the Holocaust to be a paradigm case of historical facts the denial of which precludes a rational evaluation of an important range of conceptions of human good. I conclude that this is an opinion that ought not to be tolerated in any local community, that to tolerate it is a form of vice, and that those who express it ought to be silenced.

George P. Fletcher has argued against this conclusion by remarking that:

> If it is a crime to deny the Holocaust, then perhaps it should be a crime to question the reigning view of historians about other troubling historical events. What if someone could show that Lincoln did not care about emancipating the slaves, that he was interested only in the economic value of the Union? Should this view be suppressed? This is the slope that becomes too slippery to stop the slide towards ever more censorship'.[6]

The argument is a familiar one and about it two things need to be said. The first is that it would be a good deal more compelling if its protagonists were able to supply a number of historical examples of slopes down which this kind of slide had in fact taken place, instead of merely asking 'What if?' questions. Without such examples the slippery slide into intolerance of the otherwise tolerant is in danger of seeming no more than a phantom of the liberal imagination. Secondly, Fletcher has indeed warned us of a danger of which we need to be aware and about which we need to be vigilant. But this kind of vigilance is one aspect of the virtue of prudence, a virtue required in all rational debate and practice. I conclude therefore that the slippery slope argument does not warrant the conclusion that those who deny the Holocaust ought to be allowed to voice their opinion. But how then should they be silenced, if not by government?

The answer is that they should be silenced by the same methods or by a further and more extreme development of those methods by which those real individuals whose opinions resemble those of the fictitious Rumpelstiltskin are silenced. That is to say, it should be the mark of any form of local discussion or enquiry that has any pretension to genuine practical rationality that its participants exclude the expression of this thought. And they should also treat the will to make such assertions as a sign of a character that has unfitted itself for participation in rational discussion or enquiry. Those who make them should be excluded, so far as is possible, not only from decision-making discussion, but also from holding any position in such types of local community as schools or colleges. But of course whether or not to enforce such an exclusion, whether or not to refuse to tolerate the expression of this belief, is itself something open to rational debate and enquiry for any group for whom this issue arises. It is their reasoning about particular cases, not my generalisations, which has to be conclusive.

It does of course follow from what I have said that, although the state must tolerate, it must not be allowed to impose tolerance on others. Local communal autonomy requires the freedom to make one's own decisions about where the line is to be drawn between tolerable and intolerable utterance. Such local autonomy has to extend to those institutions that are integral to local community, among them schools and colleges. And so I reiterate a conclusion plainly at odds with some of Mill's most heartfelt convictions. Yet in fact the relationship of this exclusionary and intolerant view to Mill's plea for tolerance is a little more complex. For these disagreements with Mill, fundamental though they may be, not only co-exist with but possibly derive from even more fundamental agreements. Mill rightly laid great stress on what he called 'the intelligent and living apprehension of truth', and he understood that such intelligent and living apprehension can only emerge from some systematic process of enquiry in the course of which we are held accountable by others for the reasons which we give for asserting our conclusions. The examples that Mill gives of such processes of enquiry are the dialectical interrogations of Socrates and the process of arguments and counter-arguments in medieval scholastic disputations. (Mill's praise for the latter is qualified by his disapproval of the part played by appeals to authority in such disputations; I suspect, however, that he had misunderstood what was involved in such appeals.) What is important about such face-to-face encounters is that in them we cannot evade responsibility for our assertions; we show ourselves as deserving of a hearing only in so far as we have made ourselves accountable in this way. And Mill himself provides an admirable example of someone who in very different contexts exhibited the virtues of conversational and argumentative accountability.

One mark of the possession of those virtues is that of taking pleasure in having been shown to be mistaken, something notoriously difficult to achieve. Another closely related mark is that of being both able to recognise and willing to admit that one has been shown to be mistaken. Conversely it is a failure in respect of those virtues to be unable to recognise or unwilling to admit this, a failure in respect of accountability and therefore something that *prima facie* disqualifies one from further participation in rational discourse and enquiry. Whether in a given case this should be more than a *prima facie* verdict, whether an offender's exclusions should be from only one type of discourse and enquiry or should instead extend more widely, and whether it should be a temporary or a permanent exclusion will all vary with the circumstances of the case. But it is because accountability is important in just the ways on which Mill lays emphasis that there are some beliefs failure to abandon which in the face of the evidence justifies, so long as it is continued, exclusion from the company of rational human beings.

Unsolved problems

Toleration then, so I have argued, is not in itself a virtue and too inclusive a toleration is a vice. Toleration is an exercise of virtue just in so far as it serves the purposes of a certain kind of rational enquiry and discussion, in which the expression of conflicting points of view enables us through constructive conflict to achieve certain individual and communal goods. And intolerance is also an exercise of virtue when and in so far as it enables us to achieve those same goods. But such intolerance has perhaps to extend somewhat further than I have so far suggested.

The rationality of local communities, when it exists, is always an achievement, the outcome of a history in which a variety of difficulties and obstacles has had to be overcome. And rationality in such communities is always threatened by the seductive and coercive forces that are so powerful in the wider arenas of the civil society of advanced modernity. The rational making of decisions in everyday life has to be undertaken for the most part in milieus in which individuals and groups are exposed by the technologies of the mass media to too much information of too many different types of doubtful provenance, often misleadingly abbreviated, and designed in any case to arouse short-term interest or excitement that can easily be displaced by the next targeted stimulus. It is a commonplace that the use of slogans, the shortening of the public's attention span, and the manipulation of feelings are now carried through in the media, in political debate and in advertising with extraordinary professional expertise. So a set of further problems has been created. The rhetorical modes of rational enquiry and discussion are deeply incompatible with the rhetorical modes of the dominant political and commercial culture. And we cannot confront this incompatibility and the conflicts that it generates, and the goods that it threatens, without rethinking even further some well-established notions of freedom of expression and of toleration. But about how to do this constructively in defence of the rational politics of local community no one has yet known what to say. Nor do I.

Notes

1. What I say about both Locke and Mill on toleration is highly selective; for a broader account see Susan Mendus, *Toleration and the Limits of Liberalism*, London, Macmillan, 1989, Chs 2 and 3.

2. John Locke, *Essay on Toleration*, as quoted in John Dunn, *Locke*, Oxford, Oxford University Press, 1984, p. 26.
3. *A Third Letter Concerning Toleration*. See Maurice Cranston, *John Locke*, New York, Macmillan, 1957, pp. 331–2 and 366–8.
4. John Stuart Mill, *On Liberty*, Harmondsworth, Penguin, 1978, p. 76.
5. Ibid.
6. George P. Fletcher, 'The Instability of Tolerance', in David Heyd (ed.), *Toleration: An Elusive Virtue,* Princeton, N. J., Princeton University Press, 1996, p. 167.

Index